SEASHORE SEAFOOD
how to catch it, cook it and prepare it

Keith Dawson

Copyright ©, K. Dawson, 1994

All Rights Reserved. No part of this publication may be reproduced, stored in a retrieval system, or transmitted in any form or by any means - electronic, mechanical, photocopying, recording, or otherwise - without prior written permission from the publisher.

Published by
Sigma Leisure - an imprint of Sigma Press, 1 South Oak Lane, Wilmslow, Cheshire SK9 6AR, England.

British Library Cataloguing in Publication Data
A CIP record for this book is available from the British Library.

ISBN: 1-85058-424-9

Typesetting and Design by: Sigma Press, Wilmslow, Cheshire.

Cover design: Design House

Printed by: Manchester Free Press

General Disclaimer: while due care has been taken in the preparation of this book, neither the publisher nor the author accept any responsibility for errors or omissions.

Contents

Introduction	1
Saving Money on Seafood	1
Is it safe to eat?	2
Tides	3
Warnings	5
Licences and Size Limits	6
Seafood Varieties	7
Winkles	8
Cockles	10
Mussels	13
Razor Fish	16
Shrimps	20
Prawns	23
Brown Crabs	28
Velvet Crabs	32
Lobsters	34
Sand Eels	41
Whitebait	44
Flounders	48

Occasional Discoveries   51
   Whelks   51
   King Cockles   52
   Horse Mussels   53
   Scallops   53
   Oysters   54
   Spider Crabs   54
   Dogfish   55
   Conger Eel   56

Seaweeds   58
   Carragheen   58
   Laver   59
   Dulce   59

Snorkelling   61

Setting Shore Nets   63

Bylaws   67

Seashells   69

Crab and Lobster Shells as Ornaments   70

Clothing and Footwear   73

More Warnings!   75

Not So Pleasant Finds   77

Legal Size Limits   80

Sea Fisheries Committee Offices   82

Introduction

For most people, the place to find shellfish is on the chiller shelves of the local supermarket. But traditionally, the best place of all is on the beach - so what could be more enjoyable than combining the fun of a seaside holiday with the excitement of hunting for your own food? You might be surprised at what can be found - the varieties of shellfish collectable or catchable at places around the shores of Britain include:

Winkles, cockles, mussels, razor fish, shrimps, prawns, brown crabs, velvet crabs and - the prince of shellfish - the lobster.

In this book, you'll learn how to find or catch these delicacies, plus quite a few more occasional discoveries to titillate the taste buds.

Saving Money on Seafood

Seafoods are very expensive for a number of reasons:

- High demand, particularly on the Continent
- Limited supply
- High capital and/or labour costs in collection or capture
- Most seafoods are best eaten fresh as they do not freeze well
- Highly labour-intensive preparation
- Short shelf life of the prepared product, even when kept chilled.

There are three ways to reduce the high cost of seafood:

- ☐ Buy it freshly cooked, but unprepared, and dress it yourself
- ☐ Buy it uncooked and cook and prepare it
- ☐ By far the cheapest is to go out and collect or catch it yourself. This can be good fun, good exercise and also keeps the family occupied when the weather is not suitable for lounging on the beach.

There is a great sense of achievement when tucking into absolutely fresh seafood that you have caught yourself. The enjoyment is enhanced by the fact that you know it is fresh, has been properly cooked and is carefully prepared. There is no grit in your cockles or mussels, no bits of shell in your dressed crab. Prawns in particular, caught, cooked, peeled and eaten the same day, bear no resemblance to the commercial product, usually bought frozen.

Is it safe to eat?

There is a widely-held misconception that some shellfish have poisonous bits within them. This is not so, but certain parts of some are not nice to eat. Of course, any seafood can make you ill if it is not fresh or is contaminated, but this applies to all types of food.

Tides

Knowledge of the size and times of the tides at the location you propose to visit is essential. This information and other interesting and useful data is contained in the small booklet - *Lavers' Liverpool Tide Tables*. These are widely available, costing about 90p, from most angling shops and seaside book shops. If you have difficulty in obtaining a copy, telephone the publishers on 051-709-1465. Tide tables are published by other sources, but I find these the easiest to use and conveniently pocket-sized.

While giving the heights and times of tides at Liverpool, they also provide a list of tidal time differences for numerous points around the coastline. These will be plus or minus so many hours and minutes and, added to or subtracted from the Liverpool time, will give you accurate data for your locality. If your exact locality is not listed, take the times for the nearest points that are listed each side of you and average the two.

These tables will not only tell you when the tide is in and out, but how far out it will go, which is of great importance. Some species can be found with the tide only partly out, but generally speaking, the lower the tide the better.

Heights of tides

The size of the tide varies in a four-weekly cycle, with large or Spring tides every two weeks and small or neap tides a week after each Spring tide. The overall height of the Spring tides varies through the year, with the largest occurring in Spring and Autumn.

Spring tides not only come in the furthest, but also go out furthest and these are the ones to pick for the species only found furthest out, namely razor fish, edible crabs and lobsters.

Try to get to the beach at least one hour before the predicted time of low water and work your way out as the tide ebbs. From the predicted time of low water there is approximately 30 minutes of slack water, when the tide is neither ebbing or flowing. On big Spring tides it always seems to flow back in faster than it ran out.

The author in hot (cold?) pursuit!

Warnings

BEWARE: please heed these warnings as the seashore can be a dangerous place for the unwary.

Start to retreat 30 minutes after the predicted time of low water, even if the tide is not obviously running in. Do not wade across channels to sand banks or low water exposed rock outcrops, after the tide has stopped falling. If you become engrossed in what you are doing you can easily forget the 30 minutes of slack water and find yourself cut off. If an onshore wind gets up and the sea starts to get rough, remember that this will accelerate the incoming tide.

Take local advice where available, look out for and obey any warning notices on the foreshore and use your own common sense. The golden rule is: IF IN DOUBT, DON'T.

As previously stated, there are no poisonous parts in any seafood, but you can become ill if you eat shellfish contaminated by sewage or not cooked and chilled quickly enough.

Never collect or catch anywhere near a sewage outfall. In the case of filter feeding cockles, mussels and razor fish I only collect in the colder months from October to March, but you will be safe taking them at any time of the year if commercial fishermen are taking them, as they will have been checked for purity by the Sea Fisheries officers before commercial exploitation is licensed.

Licences and Size Limits

Although commercial shell fishermen have to be licensed, the public has a right to take a reasonable quantity for their own use or to give away, but not to sell.

The public are, however, subject to the same bye-laws with regard to size limits as the commercial fisherman. These minimum size limits are strictly enforced by the Area Sea Fisheries bailiffs, particularly in the case of edible crabs and lobsters. Fines for retaining undersized specimens are considerable.

A list of these sizes is given at the back of this book and is up to date as of 1993. As time goes by, these sizes may be revised upwards as a method of conservation. Generally speaking the minimum size is set to ensure that the creature has had the opportunity to breed at least once.

Seafood Varieties

The varieties of shellfish and other seafoods collectable or catchable around our shores are dealt with in detail in the following pages.

These are just some of the delicacies you can catch. The platter includes: lobster; large brown and small velvet crabs; in front are prawns with, either side, razor fish, cockles and winkles; to the rear are mussels and, on top of the crabs, whelks.

Seashore Seafood

Winkles

These are small grey brown sea snails with a pointed top to the shell found clinging to rocks from about the half tide mark outwards, where they graze the algae on the rocks and fronds of seaweed. A really good specimen will be about the size of the end joint of your thumb.

A handful of winkles

They are in season throughout the year but are far more abundant during the Summer months. The only other sea snails found in conjunction with winkles are dog whelks and lesser or greater top shells.

Winkles are pointed on top and round in form and vary from mid-grey to very dark brown. Dog whelks are more oval and elongated and are from white to pale brown in colour and often have an orange tint around the shell opening.

Lesser top shells are round and squat, like an inverted spinning top, hence their name. They are usually greenish grey in colour showing mother of pearl iridescence around the opening. Greater top shells are, as their name implies, larger - up to about one and a quarter inches across. They are pinky brown in colour, often hum-bug striped and are usually only found far out at the extreme limits of a very low tide, but they can be swept inshore in a severe storm. The dog whelk and the top shells are not poisonous, but do not make good eating.

Catching

Collect in a bucket and transport home dry. At home, wash well in clean cold water, drain off and cook within 12 hours. Until cooked, keep the bucket in a cool place and cover with a damp cloth or a board. If you don't cover them, they will crawl out and travel a surprising distance.

Cooking

To cook, drop into boiling, lightly salted water, return to the boil and simmer for five to six minutes. Drain off and rinse under cold running water to wash away any sand or grit that may remain. Eat straight away or store refrigerated for up to 48 hours in a sealed container or plastic bag.

Preparing

To remove the winkle from its shell, use a large pin or darning needle. Push this into the flesh and remove the flesh from the shell by pulling with the pin and at the same time turning the shell. The small horny disc, known as the operculum, which closes the entrance to the shell, may have fallen off in the cooking process. If it is still attached to the meat it will pull off quite easily.

The traditional way to eat winkles is straight off the pin, dipped in salt and vinegar and accompanied by brown bread and butter if you wish to make more of a meal out of them. Winkles are certainly not to everybody's taste, but they are well worth a try, especially if washed down with a glass of beer or a white wine of your choice. In a Parisian restaurant, a saucer-full costs about £5.

Cockles

The only fairly round bivalve mollusc with ribbed shells, about one to two inches across, likely to be found just buried in sand or silt. They vary in colour from light to dark brown and from light grey to dark blue grey. They are usually found in wide sandy and slightly muddy estuaries, buried from half to one and a half inches below the surface.

Catching

To collect sufficient for your own use the only equipment required is two buckets and a small garden rake. I use a four-pronged hand rake with curved tines and draw this towards me through the silt. You will soon know if there are cockles present as it will feel as if you are hitting pebbles in the silt and some of them will flip up to the surface.

Collect until the cockles are about four inches deep in one bucket, then wash off the sand and silt and transfer to the other bucket. Repeat this process until you have a full bucket of washed cockles. I use three-gallon builders' buckets, with a wooden or plastic grip on the wire handle.

The reason for the two buckets will soon become apparent when you start to carry your catch back to the car. Two half full buckets are easier to carry than one full one and the wide grip on the handle stops your fingers going dead quite as quickly as a thin one.

If you collect your cockles from an area where there is no water left to wash them off, you have two choices. Either bring them home dirty, which entails carrying quite a lot of heavy silt home, or take a small garden riddle and sieve the bulk of the silt off. A three-gallon bucket of cockles will yield enough meat for a good feed for eight people.

Do not leave the bucket in the sun or in a hot car for any length of time. On arrival home, wash off in cold water and either cook straight away or leave covered in fresh cold water until the next day. If you wish, you can sprinkle a handful of fine oatmeal into the water they are to stand in, but I have found this to make no detectable difference to the finished product. Discard any shells that are open and do not shut tight when tapped.

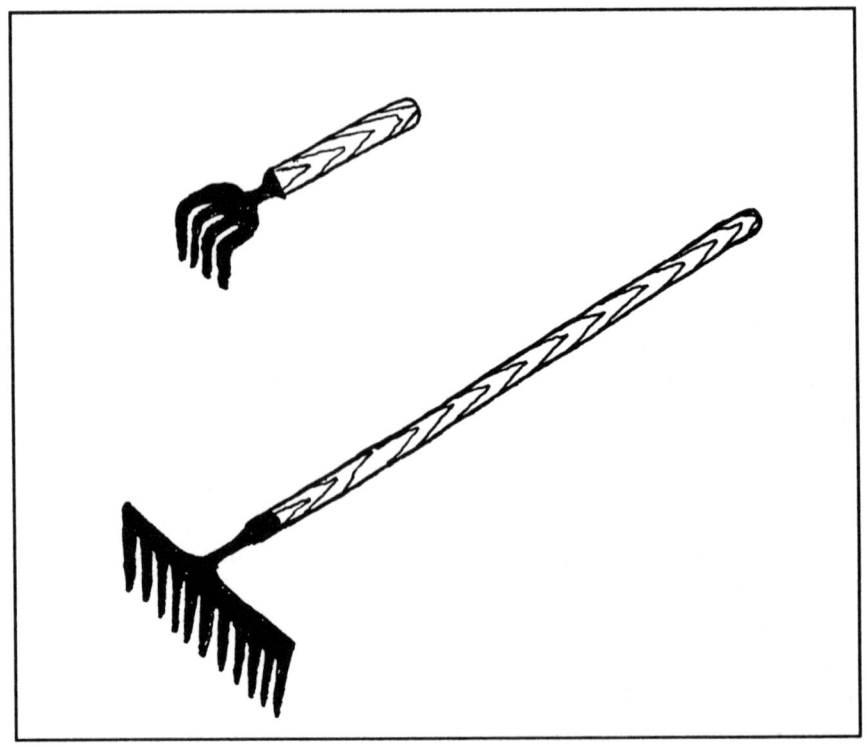

Single-handed and double-handed cockle rakes. Widths are four inches and twelve inches respectively

A haul of cockles collected with a single-handed rake

Cooking

To cook, use a large, lidded pan or a pressure cooker. Put about half an inch of water in the pan and add cockles until about two thirds full. This is because the volume increases as the shells open. Bring to the boil with the lid firmly on and simmer for five minutes, with steam coming out round the lid. They will not boil dry as the shells release a lot of water as they open. If using a pressure cooker, bring up to pressure and cook for two minutes at full pressure.

Preparing

Dunk in cold water to stop them over cooking and becoming rubbery. Flip the meat out of the opened shells into a colander and rinse it thoroughly and quite roughly a number of times in bowls of cold water until you are getting little or no sediment of sand or silt collecting at the bottom of the bowl. Do this rinsing in small batches, not the lot at once.

You will now have a large bowl of beautifully fresh, grit free cockles which you can keep for up to 48 hours in the refrigerator either as they are or marinating in vinegar. I prefer to dilute the vinegar with one part water to two parts vinegar and add a little salt to the liquid, rather than sprinkle the salt on when eating, but this is obviously a matter of personal taste. Cockles have a fairly strong odour, so store in a sealed container or bag.

Cockles are usually eaten cold, but they can be used as one of the seafoods on a *fruits de Mer* pizza, in a paella or they can be tossed in seasoned flour or fine oatmeal and quickly deep fried and eaten with a squeeze of lemon juice. Also, try them tossed in hot garlic butter.

Mussels

These are found adhering to rocks or gravel beds, usually in sheltered locations in bays and estuaries.

Mussels, of all shellfish, have the worst reputation for making people ill. There are two reasons for this: they will grow in badly polluted water and they spoil quickly if not kept cool between collection and cooking.

There is no truth in the common belief that there is a poisonous moss inside a mussel. In many, but not all mussels, there is a bunch of hair-like filaments, sometimes called the beard, growing out of the body. These filaments protrude from the shell and attached the mussel to a rock or pebble and often to its neighbours.

I repeat, these filaments are not poisonous, but are certainly not nice to eat. They can be pulled out after cooking. If you buy uncooked mussels from a fishmonger's, they will probably have few or no attachment filaments, as the mussels will probably have been transferred when very small from their original position to commercial beds. Once moved, they do not grow new attachments.

Catching

I have been collecting mussels from local rocks for many years, from October to March and I have never made anybody ill. Only collect where you see local people collecting or from obviously clean locations, remote from any sewage outfalls. Discard any that are not tightly shut. All you need to collect them is a bucket and if your hands are soft, a pair of old gloves, as they can be quite hard to pull from the rocks and the shell can be sharp at the broad end. Two buckets are a good idea if they have to be carried for any distance.

After collecting, do not leave in the sun or a warm car. Transport home without water, but soon after arrival wash off with cold water and either cook straight away or leave covered with fresh cold water until the following day.

Freshly gathered mussels

Cooking

Before cooking, again check for any that are open and discard any that will not close tight when tapped. Cook exactly the same as cockles, but you will find that they do not come out of the shell as easily as cockles. The mussel meat usually stays attached to one half of the shell and if you try pulling it out you usually leave a large lump attached to the shell. The easiest way to remove the meat without damage is to pull away the half shell to which it is not attached and use the broad end of this as a scoop, to scrape the meat away from its attachment.

Preparing

Once free of the shell, hold the meat hollow side up, between the bunched fingertips and hold it under a slightly running cold tap. This will wash out any bits of gravel or shell in the hollow of the body and also expose the attachment point of the anchor filaments near the base of the tongue like structure. Grip these filaments with the fingertips of the other hand, as close to their base as possible and pull sharply. This will pull a lump of meat out of the middle of the mussel. This is not catastrophic and can usually be prevented by closing the fingertips of the hand holding the mussel to leave only a very small aperture through which to pull the filaments. These should come away in a bunch, attached to a little lump, leaving a small hole looking just like a navel.

Occasionally you may find a minute, pea-sized orange and white crab inside the mussel. I discard these mussels as the flesh is often distorted by the crab and an even smaller male crab is often present and hard to spot.

The cooked mussels will vary in colour from white, through cream to yellow and sometimes quite a bright orange. This is quite normal, but I discard any grey or dark brown ones as these are not in good condition. I also discard any shrivelled or distorted ones.

If, while handling the meat, you see any small blemish on the smooth mantle, this could well be a tiny pearl embedded in the flesh. Pop it out between your thumb nails. Most of these will be the size of a pin head, but can occasionally be nearly the size of a match-head. The incidence of pearls varies from location to location. I would expect to find a dozen pearls in a bucket full of mussels from my local rocks. Other than for interest, you do not have to search for and remove pearls, as you will probably find them when chewing the mussel.

Give the prepared meat a final rinse, drain and store refrigerated for up to 48 hours, as for cockles.

Eat cold with salt and vinegar to taste or toss in hot garlic butter. Refer to a good recipe book for many other alternatives.

Razor Fish

Most people who have walked the tide-line of any large sandy beach will be familiar with the shell of the razor fish. For anybody who does not know what one looks like, they can be up to six inches long and similar to the blade of an old-fashioned cut throat razor.

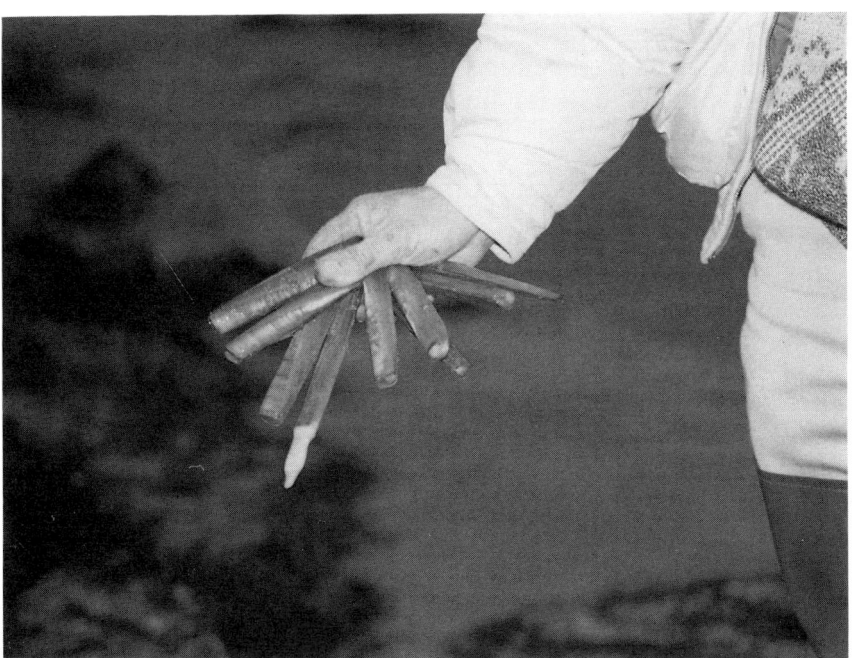

Razor fish and shells

What you find washed up on the beach is, of course, only one half of the shell of this bivalve mollusc.

You will find the live razor fish only near the extreme low water mark on sandy beaches. Their presence is fairly easily spotted. They lie vertically in the sand with their top just below the surface. The only indication of their presence is a slight dimple in the surface of the sand. When disturbed they will dive down to a depth of 12 to 18 inches below the surface. When they do this they often emit a jet of water into the air and always leave behind an oval shaped hole full of water.

Catching

To stand any chance of catching them you must be the first person to walk on that stretch of sand after the tide has receded. If someone has walked before you, the razor fish will all have dived for the depths. If there is a line of footprints, keep clear of them by at least six feet.

There are various methods of capture, but first you have to locate them. To do this, pick really low tides, say, those of one foot or less above datum and either calm conditions or, even better, an off-shore wind which will take the water further out. Follow the tide out for, say, the last 15 minutes of its ebb, walking where the water has just left. Walk five paces and then stamp your feet. Look out for water spouts or the sudden appearance of oval holes about three quarters of an inch long. Proceed along the beach in this manner until you find signs, working your way out with the tide.

Razor fish are usually in colonies or beds, so once you know where they are, you can return to the best places time and again. On a good bed there may be as many as half a dozen or more per square yard.

The most challenging way to catch them is bare-handed. To do this you must proceed slowly and place you feet down very lightly looking for the slight dimple they leave in the surface of the sand. When you see a likely dimple quietly bend down and turn your dominant hand palm upwards. Cross your thumb and little finger over the palm and hold your remaining three fingers tightly together, straight and stiff. Thrust these into the sand as quickly as possibly, about two or three inches from the dimple and at a downward angle of about 30 degrees.

The aim is to get your finger tips about 1 inch or more below sand level by the time they reach a point immediately below the dimple. The dimple may have been caused by a sand-worm, a sea urchin or a razor fish. If you feel nothing, it was a sand-worm, while a scrunch, like breaking a weak eggshell, means it was a sea urchin. If you hit something hard it is a razor fish.

Gently retrieving a razor fish

The moment you feel this hard object, exert a horizontal pressure and do not release this pressure for a second. With your other hand excavate the sand away from your fingers until you can grip the top of the shell securely between your thumb and first finger. Now excavate more sand and at the same time pull firmly but gently upwards. If you pull too hard the fleshy foot will break off. Be patient, keep up a firm but gently upward pull and after a little while the foot will relax and the whole razor fish will be in your hand. The foot, or more accurately, the digger, will be dangling out of the bottom end of the shell, but it will soon retract.

When digging down to the trapped shell with your free hand, dig a little from the side as the top of the shell can cut your finger if you dig straight down from above.

I must admit that hand capture is a bit of an acquired art and there are easier ways of catching these elusive creatures, particularly if you require a fair number.

The quickest method is to proceed along the beach, stamping your feet every yard or so and the moment you spot a water spout or hole insert a garden fork to its full depth about 6 inches from the hole. Do this as quickly as possible with the fork nearly vertical and the moment it is at full depth, pull the handle towards you. This will compress the sand and prevent the razor fish diving any deeper.

You can now firmly and slowly push the fork over to lift the sand and you will usually find the shell. If it is not in the first fork full, forget it - they are much quicker diggers than humans. This method does break quite a few shells, which does not matter if you are going to prepare them quickly, but discard the broken ones, if not.

Another simple method, which breaks fewer shells, is to take a long-bladed knife and when you see a hole, insert the blade into the sand to one side of the hole at an angle of about 45 degrees and sweep sideways towards the hole. The blade should strike the shell and a lateral pressure will hold the shell in place while you dig down with your free hand or a small trowel. If your knife is sharp, too great a side pressure may well cut the shell in half.

The final method of capture is part of seaside folklore and I must confess I have not tried it out. For those of an enquiring nature, proceed as follows:

Take a packet of salt and a tea spoon. Place a spoonful of salt into each hole that appears. Do this to as many holes as you can find or until you run out of salt. Go back to where you started and the shells are supposed to pop up out of the sand of their own volition.

Cooking

Razor fish require virtually no cooking. Rinse in cold water to remove sand, drain and place in a large pan or in the sink with the plug in. Pour boiling water over the shells and they will pop open almost immediately. Pour off the water or pull out the plug as soon as they have opened. The longer they cook, the tougher they get.

Preparing

The French prize them open with a knife and eat them live. I only eat the foot or digger - nip this off just below its junction with the body. Eaten nearly raw this is white and tender. Sprinkle with a little salt and vinegar.

In addition to being good to eat, razor fish are excellent bait for sea fishing, either from a boat or for beach casting, where the muscular foot stays on the hook well.

Shrimps

The brown shrimp is a delicious little morsel that can be caught in a simple push net usually in shallow estuarial waters with a silty, sandy bottom. Search for them in the shallow channels or pools left as the tide recedes. Take care not to be cut off by the incoming tide.

Catching

A three-foot-wide semicircular push net with a six- or seven-foot handle is ideal. A bigger net is awkward to transport and harder to push. The mesh needs to be small, say a quarter of an inch square for the main net, which should be tapered down to an end sock of even smaller mesh. The end sock should be open ended, but tied closed with an attached cord.

Take a large canvas or strong plastic shoulder bag, slung across your body and hanging at hip level. Make sure it has small drainage holes or you will end up carrying a lot of water as well as your shrimps. Push the net ahead of you, with the flat bar pressed firmly against the bottom. This requires the use of both hands, hence the need for the shoulder bag. If the handle of the net is too short, you will have difficulty avoiding treading on the trailing sock end.

Check the contents of the sock end periodically and empty when required by standing the net, pushing the handle end into the sand. Place the end of the sock into the shoulder bag and undo the knotted cord.

In some places you may be lucky and catch a few prawns among the shrimps, particularly if you are near rocks. You may also catch

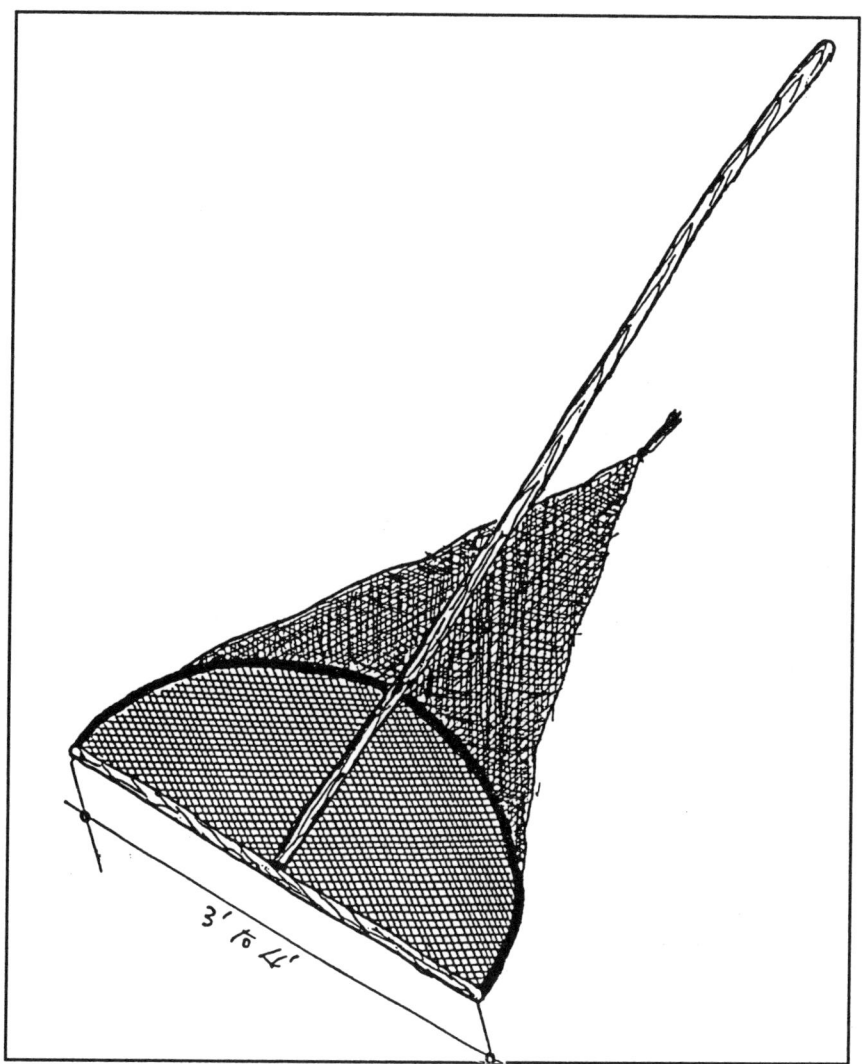

Hand-pushed shrimp net. Make the handle about six to eight feet long and use a maximum mesh size of about a quarter of an inch. Tie the opening end as shown.

the occasional flat fish, usually flukes or flounders. These are a bonus as they are excellent to eat, if large enough.

Cooking

Shrimps must be cooked as soon as possible and certainly not longer than two hours after capture. The shrimp boats cook them on board, as they would spoil if they were kept uncooked until return to port.

If you have to travel any distance to catch your shrimps, it is a good idea to take a boiling pan with you and sufficient fresh water. You can either boil your catch on a driftwood fire or take a gas bottle and boiling ring.

Bring the water to the boil and drop your shrimps in. Return to the boil and simmer for two minutes. If you have a good catch, it is better to cook them in batches, rather than one big pan full, as this will take too long to return to the boil and some of them will over-cook. To facilitate batch cooking, have a wire mesh basket in the pan to lift out the cooked shrimps. This must be of small mesh to retain the shrimps. Spread the cooked shrimps out to cool or dunk in cold water. Place the cooled, cooked shrimps in a bucket or other plastic container and cover. Keep cool and eat the same day or store in the refrigerator for up to 48 hours, or in the freezer for up to one month.

Preparing

Preferably pick, that is, shell your shrimps before freezing, as this radically reduces their volume for storage and they shell more easily when fresh than when they have been frozen.

In fact, easy is a very relative term when it comes to picking shrimps. Fresh they are difficult and tedious, over-cooked or frozen they will try the patience of a saint. The time involved in picking them accounts for their scarcity and their terrible price.

Professional pickers will shell at the rate of about one per second or faster. When you first start you will do well to peel one in 10 seconds, but with a but of practice you should be able to get this down to five seconds or less.

Take the head of the shrimp in the fingers of your non-dominant hand with the back uppermost, leaning slightly away from you and its tail pointing towards your dominant hand. Grasp the tail portion between your first two fingers and thumb and push the body slightly into the back of the head. Now pull gently away, with a slightly twisting motion and the tail section of the shell should come away, leaving the flesh attached to the head. Pull the flesh away from the head. If they are over-cooked or have not been cooked soon enough, the flesh will come away from the head and remain inside the tail section. This makes the job slower, as you will have to peel at least one ring of shell off the tail section before you can pull the meat out and it will probably break.

Eat fresh with salt and vinegar to taste, in a sauce or as a garnish to other fish dishes.

Potted shrimps are absolutely delicious. Place a lightly salted portion of picked shrimps in a ramekin or other small heat-proof container and pour on melted butter to just cover. Allow to cool and set. Store in the fridge for up to four days or in the freezer for up to one month. Eat at room temperature or slightly warmed, with salad or spread on thin brown bread. All the fiddling suddenly becomes worthwhile.

Prawns

The prawn, when fully grown, is much larger than the shrimp and is pinky-orange when cooked.

Look for them under rocks or rocky ledges, particularly those with seaweed hanging from them. You will find them under rocks when the tide is about two thirds out, down to low water mark and the lower the tide the better.

Catching

Go prawning on the two or three days preceding the lowest tide and you will be able to reach further out each day. The prawns tend to retreat outwards as the tides get progressively lower - they don't like being left beneath rocks that have no water under them.

You need a net of a quarter inch mesh or less and preferably of a dark colour. Black, dark brown or dark green are best, as prawns when disturbed, swim at amazing speed for the nearest seaweed. Many mistake a dark net for seaweed and most obligingly dive straight in.

The net frame needs to be of strong metal, say a quarter inch diameter steel or one eighth by half inch flat iron bar, bent into an oval, or more precisely, a heart shape, with the more pointed end away from the handle. The frame should be about 14 to 18 inches from handle attachment to point and 12 to 15 inches across at its widest point. The frame should be securely fixed into a hole in the end of a strong wooden broom handle about five feet long.

Alternatively, the frame can be carried about six inches up each side of the handle. In either case, bind well with copper wire to secure and prevent splitting. If the frame becomes stuck under a rock it needs to be well secured to the handle or when you pull you may well lose it.

Secure the net to the frame with looped copper wire. The wire needs to be fairly strong, say 1mm in diameter, or it will wear through too quickly on the rough rocks. Hang the net below the frame by the looped wire as the frame will then protect the net from wear. You can buy ready-made nets, but they are expensive

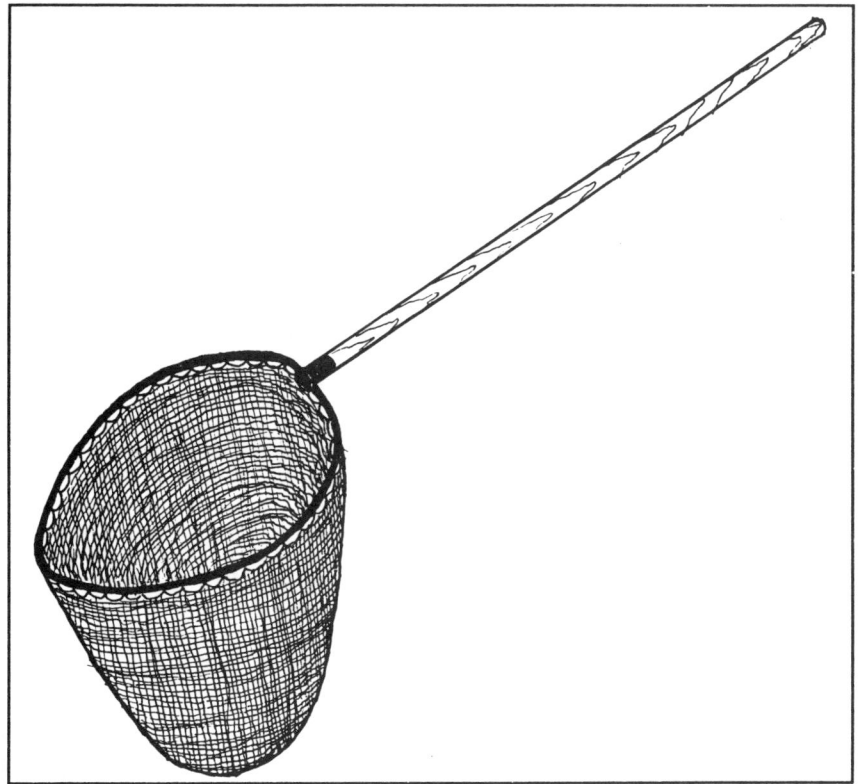

Prawn net. The handle is five to six feet long; the net is 14 inches to 18 inches long and is 12 inches to 15 inches in both depth and width. Use a quarter-inch mesh.

and often have the net looped over the frame, You will be lucky to get more than a couple of trips before major repairs are necessary.

The net should be 12 to 15 inches deep, as prawns are highly active and will often jump out of a shallow net before you can get them into your shoulder bag or other container. A shoulder bag is best as it leaves both hands free. Either tip the prawns out of the net or get hold of them where the tail joins the head. They are nearly impossible to hold by the tail and the front of the head has a sharp, protective, saw-edged spike.

You will find a multitude of other marine life in your net. Return these to the water by gently inverting the net and waiting for them to untangle themselves.

You may occasionally catch a keepable-sized brown crab and sometimes disturb a lobster, which will usually shake your net, then swim off rapidly. For what to do if you can still see and follow the lobster, see later under Lobsters.

Start about one hour before low water and follow the tide out. Pick rocks that still have water around them, as the prawns hang upside down on the underside of the rock or cling to clumps of seaweed that hang from the side of the rock. Once the water has receded completely, the prawns will have retreated to the furthest small crevices and can not be reached with the net. If you are bold by nature and desperate for prawns you can try pulling them out by hand from small holes that have dried out, leaving sometimes quite amazing numbers of prawns stranded. There is one such hole on my local beach which regularly yields half a pound or more, if conditions are right and nobody has beaten you to it. I've seen two locals risking broken bones to get there first.

Approach each rock quietly and thrust the net as far as possible under the rock keeping the net low to the sea-bed. When it won't go any further, lift the net until the point is touching the rock and the base is a little way off, then withdraw quickly and the prawns will dive into the net. If seaweed is hanging from the rock, lift the net up under this from below, shaking the net and the weed as you lift it clear of the water. You can quite often hear them flapping in the weed. Keep shaking until the flapping stops or hold the net in one hand and carefully lift and shake the weed with the other.

Work around the rock and keep at it until you stop catching, then move to another. You may get nothing under one rock and a dozen or more from the next one as prawns are gregarious.

A good prawn should be three to four inches long, excluding the whiskers which can be longer than the whole body. Return the small ones, they will be much bigger next year.

Prawns usually start to appear among the tidal rocks in April and are most abundant in May and June. Their numbers then decrease and they are all back out in deep water by September or October, depending on when the Autumn gales start.

In May and June the majority will have masses of minute eggs attached to the underside of the tail section. When first laid, these are bright orange in colour. When near to hatching they change to a dark blue grey. These eggs stay attached during cooking and come away with the tail section when the prawns are picked.

The prawn's diet is a mixture of animal and vegetable matter. Prawns are fond of a type of green algae and when they have been eating this it can be seen as a green mass inside the semi-transparent body. This can look quite odd and to some people, off-putting, but it is perfectly harmless and does not affect the meat in the tail, which is all you eat.

There is a wide variation of colour among live prawns, from very pale to very dark, depending on their surroundings. Very occasionally you may catch one which, instead of being semi-transparent, is milky white inside. I don't know what causes this, but to be on the safe side I discard them.

They all turn bright orange when cooked. Provided your prawns are alive and kicking when caught, they are perfectly safe to eat.

Cooking

Cook the prawns as soon as possible after capture and certainly not longer than two hours or they will spoil. Do not worry if they have started to go milky as long as they were clear when you caught them.

Cook exactly as described for shrimps. If you have only caught a small number, place them in a dry pan, boil the kettle and pour the boiling water over them. Bring back to the boil and simmer for two minutes. This is quicker than boiling the water in the pan and adding the prawns. If you have caught a large quantity, use a larger pan with a wire basket and batch cook as for shrimps.

Proper technique for shelling a prawn. The crabs come later!

Preparing

Picking prawns is far less tedious than shrimps, because of their greater size and generally tougher shell. If you find one with a soft shell it means it has recently changed it. These soft ones are perfectly all right to eat, but are difficult to peel. Proceed as described for shelling shrimps. If the meat breaks away from the head and remains in the tail section you have cooked them for too long.

I pick prawns at the sink with the cold tap running gently. When you pull the tail meat away from the head you will often find that some of the stomach contents or unlaid eggs adhere to the front end of the meat. This is quite harmless, but I prefer to rinse it off.

If you eat your prawns soon after they are cooked, they taste totally different to those left with their shell on until the next day. Picked and eaten straight away, they have no fishy taste at all, but a sweet, nutty flavour.

The characteristic slightly fishy prawn flavour develops if they are left with their shells on for 12 to 24 hours.

As with all seafoods, store either shelled or unshelled, under refrigeration. Always shell before freezing, unless you wish to serve them later, shell on, tossed in hot garlic butter. Do not store frozen, shell on for more than one month and make sure the container they are in is air-tight. If it is not, the meat will dry out and shrivel inside the shell.

Brown Crabs

The brown crab is known as the edible crab. This is a slight misnomer in that there are other edible crabs in British waters, but certainly the brown crab is the principal edible member of the family. The reason for this is the size to which it grows and the amount of meat it contains. There is a size limit of 125mm or five inches, across the shell, from side to side, below which it is an offence under the Sea Fisheries bye-laws, to take them.

Crabs can be caught throughout the year, but tend to move into deeper water from October until March, returning to the tidal rocks as the water starts to warm up and the food supply increases.

They are found under rocks or in crevices in rocks, from about the half tide mark outwards. When the water has left they will retreat as far as they can, wedging themselves into holes or crevices, always facing outward, with their claws across their front, ready to defend themselves. Do not attempt to pull them out by hand. A small crab can inflict a painful wound and a large one can break a finger.

Catching

The equipment you require is a bucket or strong bag and a three to four foot length of galvanised straining wire about an eighth of an inch in diameter. Bend one end into a loop about one and a half inches in diameter to stop the wire pulling through your hand. Bend the other end to form a hook about one and a half inches long by about a one inch gape.

Look under rocks and ledges, particularly where there is hanging seaweed. If you can't see, rake about with the hook and listen for crunching and grating noises or you may feel one or more knocks on the hook. The noises are caused by the crab retreating and wedging itself against the underside of the rock. If you hear a lot of scurrying, scrabbling noises, these will be caused by small, inedible green shore crabs. If you can't see the crab and it gets well wedged, don't waste too much time, move on and look for more accessible ones.

When you have hooked a crab out of its lair, get hold of it from behind and above, across the widest part of the shell. A crab cannot articulate its claws to reach its back. Place it in your bucket or bag and cover it with seaweed before you put in the next one. Plenty of seaweed will stop them fighting and damaging one another.

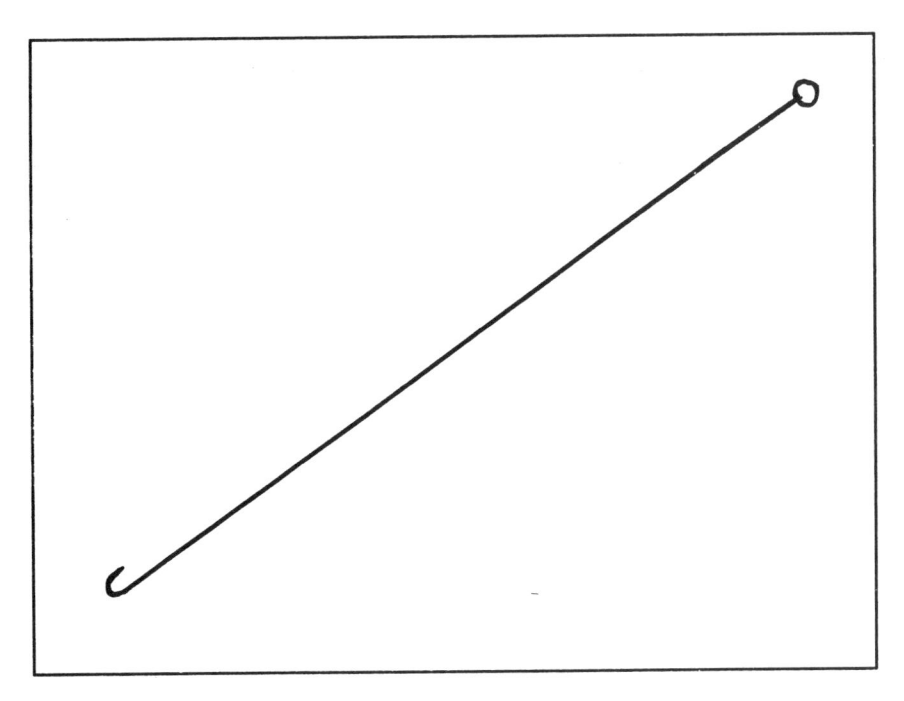

Crab and lobster hook; length - about four feet; make hook gap about one to one and a half inches; use 4mm or 5mm galvanised wire.

If the shell is at all soft it means the crab has recently changed it and the flesh will be small, soft and watery. If it is undamaged, leave it for later in the year.

The darker and more barnacle encrusted it is, the fuller it will be. Females generally have more brown meat in the body than males, who have larger claws. To tell the sex, turn the crab upside down and look at the vestigial tail, which is turned back under the abdomen to form a protective flap. In the male the tail is narrow and pointed. In the female it is much broader and rounded. If you catch more than you need, retain the dark females for preference, but keep a dark male rather than a bright female.

If you are buying crabs, ask to select your own. Check their weight size for size as some crabs have a lot of water in them and they lose this after capture, so pick the heavy ones. The difference is even more noticeable if the crabs have been cooked. Keep the crabs cool and covered with damp seaweed. Cook them within 12 hours of capture and discard any that have died.

Cooking

Drop the crabs into a large pan of slightly salted boiling water, with sufficient depth to cover them completely and return to the boil. Simmer for 10 to 15 minutes, depending on size. Pour off boiling water and run cold water over the crabs. Leave for 10 minutes to cool, then remove and leave the right way up to drain. When drained, dress the crab immediately or place in a plastic bag or box and store for up to 24 hours in the refrigerator, before dressing. Eat within 48 hours of cooking.

Preparing

To dress the cooked crab, first pull off all the legs and place these to one side. Take the body in one hand, back down and grasp the underside with the other hand with your fingers towards the tail. Pull the rear of the crab upwards and forwards and the whole centre should come out. If it is obstinate, insert the blade of a stout knife between the main shell and the tail and gently prise apart.

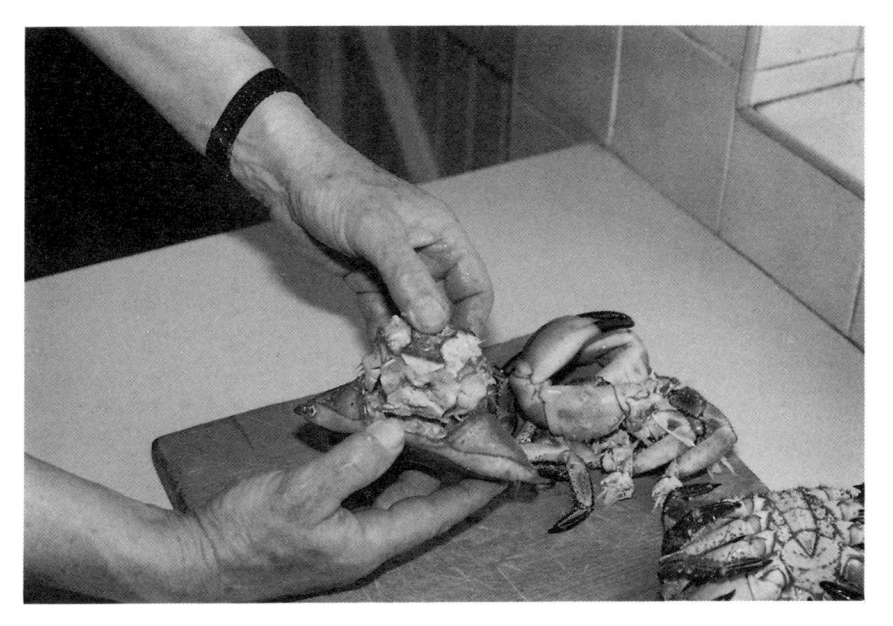

Pulling the body from the shell

Place the centre portion to one side and attend to what is left in the main shell. The mouth parts and stomach sack should be removed by a downward pressure on the mouth flaps which will cause them to break loose from the shell. A thin, semi-transparent membrane will stretch around the inside of the main shell and it is the creamy brown or yellowish paste-like substance behind this membrane that is known as the brown meat. Remove the membrane and scoop out the paste and place in a basin.

If the crab has recently changed its shell there may be little or no brown meat. If it is getting near to changing its shell it will be full, but will already have its next shell formed around the brown meat as a recognisable but soft, rubbery replica of the existing shell. Scoop the brown meat out or you may find it easier to peel the new shell off the meat. In females you may also sometimes find a dense orange mass which is unlaid eggs. Discard any rubbery shell or eggs.

Pushing mouth parts and stomach out with thumb

When the crab discards its old shell, it inflates the new, soft one with water to a considerably greater size than the one discarded. This then hardens in a few weeks and the crab grows to fill its new shell during the following 12 months.

Now take the body portion, previously laid aside and rinse under running water to wash away any adhering stomach contents. Remove the gills or dead men's fingers. These are white, frond-like pieces down each side of the body which are inedible but not poisonous. Holding the remains of the body in one hand, take a very slim-bladed knife and rake out the white flesh from the holes where the legs were attached. There is quite a lot of meat in these holes, but some very thin bone divisions between the holes form what is known as the matrix. Care must be taken to avoid breaking this thin bone. If you have plenty of crab to dress do not spend too long trying to get every bit out of the sockets. Some people prefer to remove the meat from the leg sockets before pulling the body out of the main shell.

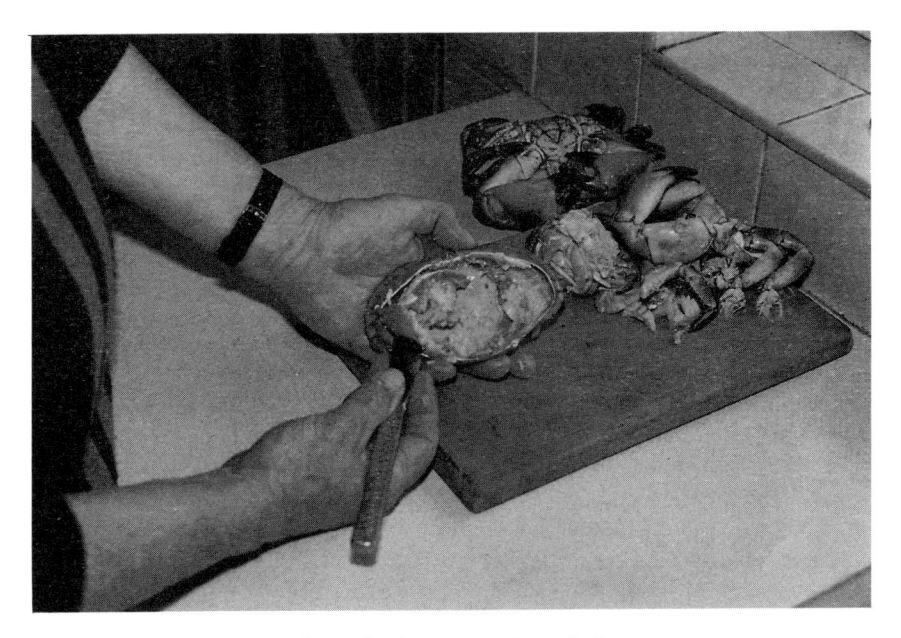

Removing brown meat from shell

Next take the small legs and crack them - I use the metal handle of a stainless steel knife. Each segment has white meat inside. It is up to you how many of these you crack as it is a tedious job, but the meat is very tasty.

Now take the front legs and claws and break these into their individual segments. Poke and rake out the meat from these sections. The claws are very thick and will have to be cracked to remove the flesh. Watch out for shell splinters and the thin, white, flat bone in the centre of the flesh.

If you wish to present the crab meat in its shell, take the back shell and break away the under-shell to the thin line where the shell splits on shedding. Scrub, wash and dry the shell. Place the white meat into it, leaving a hollow in the centre for the brown meat. If you wish, you can mix the brown meat with fine brown bread-crumbs in the proportion of two parts meat to one part crumbs, plus a little salt and pepper to taste.

I prefer to mix the brown and white meat thoroughly together, adding black pepper and a good dash of salad cream, beating the mixture up to an even past. You can return this paste to the shell and you should have enough to fill the back shell of the number of crabs you have dressed. Use the meat-filled shell as the centre piece of a salad. Alternatively, spread thickly on open rolls or batch cakes and garnish with cayenne pepper, watercress or parsley. A good crab sandwich should be two quarter-inch thick slices of brown bread with half an inch of crab in between.

Velvet Crabs

These are small greyish brown crabs, often with a touch of blue on the claws, up to about three inches across the shell. They have a velvet-like covering on the shell and their eyes turn ruby red when cooked.

They are highly prized on the Continent where the habit of sitting in a restaurant or pavement cafe fiddling with a platter of mixed seafoods is an excellent excuse for relaxing there for a couple of hours or more, watching the world go by. When I was last in Paris they were selling for the equivalent of about £1.50 each.

Catching

You will find them among the outer rocks with the brown crabs and lobsters. They are one of the varieties of swimming crabs, their back legs being flattened into paddles. They can move very quickly in water, unlike the brown crab, which is ponderous in its movements. They remain very quick moving when caught and can give a nasty nip, so it is best to tip them directly from your net into your bag or bucket. They tend to die in air rather more quickly than brown crabs, so cook as soon as possible after capture, say within four hours. Place them in plenty of damp seaweed as they are caught and transport them home in the weed, or they will fight and die more quickly.

Cooking

Cook as for brown crabs and store chilled for up to 48 hours.

Preparing

Being small they are far too laborious to dress for obtaining a reasonable amount of crab meat, but the flesh is tasty and it is well worthwhile, if you have the time to spare, sitting on your own or with friends and cracking your way through half a dozen velvets, preferably accompanied by plenty of good wine and conversation.

Lobsters

The lobster is familiar to nearly everyone, from films, from illustrations in women's magazines and on the front covers of cookery books. It is renowned for its excellent taste and high cost. All this is true, it does taste excellent and it does cost a lot. There are, however, numerous places around our coast where you can catch your own lobsters and even more places where you can buy them fresh on the quay-side. In the Summer, when they are at their most plentiful, you should be able to purchase them live, direct from the boat, for about £4 per pound. A one and a quarter to one and a half pound lobster will yield enough meat for a fine lobster salad for two persons, which puts it in the same price bracket as fillet steak.

Catching

If you live near the sea in an area where lobsters are found and have your own boat you can make or buy a few lobster pots and catch lobsters the traditional way.

By the time you have made or bought the pots, together with their ropes and marker buoys, caught or bought fish for pot bait, heaved the boat and engine up and down a steep stony beach, lost half your pots in the first storm and had the rest emptied by Hooray Henrys in speed boats, you soon realise why lobsters are so expensive.

If you are a masochist, proceed as above. If not, a far cheaper, easier and more reliable way is to catch them by hand among the outer tidal rocks. For equipment you will require a bucket or bag and a wire hook as described for crabs, plus a good sized net with a half to three quarter inch mesh. Too fine a mesh makes the net more obtrusive and difficult to move through the water with any speed.

Go looking for lobsters only on the really low tides and get there at least one hour before low water and follow the tide out.

A likely spot for a lobster!

Probe about under any rock that has a hole or space under it and remember that where the rocks lie on sand or gravel, the lobster will often dig its own hole under the rock. If is has been recently dug there will be a telltale pile of clean gravel or sand beside the rock and if the rock is still surrounded by water and you see a muddy stain in the otherwise clear water, you know that the lobster is still in the hole and still digging.

When you probe under a rock, do so gently and slowly at first. Quite often you will feel one or more sharp knocks on the hook as the lobster grapples with it. Other times you will touch its antennae

- it will move off and you will not feel a thing. When it realises that something strange has invaded its lair it will do one of two things. If the space is big enough it may retreat and stay under the rock, or it may swim slowly out to investigate what has disturbed it. At this stage it is probably more annoyed than alarmed and your movements should be quiet and slow to avoid scaring it.

A lobster in its lair

If it comes out far enough, place the net between the lobster and the rock and gently steer it away from the rock before trying to scoop it up. Lobsters can swim slowly in any direction, but only fast backwards. Once you have your lobster clear of the rock try to place the net about 6 to 12 inches behind it and then bring the hook slowly up in front of it. A light touch on its antennae or front legs will send it shooting backwards into the net.

Sometimes a lobster will shoot out from under the rock as soon as you insert the hook, quite often from the far side, so while you are probing keep on eye out all round the rock. It can just as often come out straight towards you, using any available seaweed as cover. Lobsters look quite bright blue in the water and their antennae bright red.

A lobster successfully hooked; note rod protruding above.

An alarmed lobster can swim for a short distance at considerable speed, but will usually stop within 10 feet or less. A lobster's sight is poor except at very close range, but it can distinguish fast movement and shadows at some distance and is very sensitive to vibrations. If it shoots away, do not bound after it. Follow slowly and quietly without splashing and wait for it to stop. Circle slowly to approach from the side, place the net slowly upright behind it and tap on the front with your hook.

If a lobster comes out of its hole and retreats back into it, persevere, probing gently initially and it may come out again, but not necessarily from the same place. If it does not reappear, probe much more forcefully, rattling the hook about under the rock and it will probably come out eventually. If it does not, as a last resort step back a couple of paces and wait quietly for a minute or two, watching carefully.

When all has gone quietly it may start to sneak out to head for another rock or bed of seaweed. Let it get clear of the rock before trying to net it or it will probably dive straight back under and not come out again. Even when you know there is a good lobster under a rock, if you have spent much more than five minutes trying to get it out, give up and look for others, possibly returning later, if the tide allows.

Do not try netting in water deeper than about two feet as you will have difficulty in seeing, following and netting.

On really low tides, many lobsters will be under rocks that the water has completely left. In this case you will know one is there when you feel it knock the hook or hear it flapping its tail and splashing about in what water remains in the bottom of the hole. You will rarely find anything under a rock that does not have some pooled water under it. When the water has retreated you will have to hook the lobster out by getting the tip of the hook round the body or one of the large front legs. If you can't hook it out try returning on the incoming tide, when there is about six inches of water and it may come out of its own accord or when encouraged by a gentle prod.

To get hold of a lobster, always grip it from behind and on top, towards the rear of the main body shell. It can not articulate its claws to that position. Never put your hand into a bag to remove a lobster or you may find it has removed your finger. Always tip out the contents of your bag, so that you can see what you are doing. Pack seaweed in the bag with your catch to prevent them damaging each other. You can immobilise the claws using an elastic band to hold the pincer shut. The muscle that opens the claw is far weaker than the one that closes it. When dealing with one claw, immobilise the other by placing a foot on it, or gripping it between your knees if you like living dangerously!

To illustrate the power that even a modest-sized lobster has in its claws, one of about a pound that I was carrying from the beach in a bucket, neatly clipped the stem off my father-in-law's favourite briar pipe when he gave it a prod. Not the black plastic bit, but clean through the wood, close to the bowl.

Lobsters kept damp and cool in seaweed will live for many hours, but I always cook them as soon as possible. You can store them chilled in a sealed bag for up to three days, but I prefer to eat them within 24 hours. The longer you keep them the more fishy the flavour becomes.

You can freeze lobster, either dressed or shell on for up to one month, but when thawed the flesh loses much of its juiciness, flavour and texture. It is like comparing a frozen strawberry with a fresh one.

Cooking

There are two schools of thought on the boiling of lobster: the 'place in cold water, heat slowly' method and the 'plunge into boiling water' methods.

The slow heating method relies on the theory that the lobster loses consciousness by the time the water reaches blood heat and therefore does not suffer.

The plunge into boiling water alternative relies on the fact that the lobster is killed almost immediately and not left crashing around the pan for two or three minutes or longer, while the water temperature rises to blood heat.

The slow heating method makes judging the cooking time more difficult, as the time taken up to the boil will depend on the variable factors of the volume of water being heated and the strength of the heat supply. As cooking will start well below boiling point, you may easily over-cook, particularly if you are dealing with a number of lobsters at once in a large pan containing a lot of water.

I am not convinced that the slow heating method involves no suffering and I dislike plunging a live creature of the size and complexity of a lobster, into boiling water.

I answer this dilemma by killing the lobster immediately before dropping it into boiling water. I do this by stabbing it through the top of the head with a slim, stiff, sharp pointed knife. Lie the lobster on a board, placing the point of the knife on the mid-line on the top of the shell, about a third of the way back from the eyes to the obvious cross line on the shell.

Hold the knife vertically with one hand and hit the end of the handle smartly with the other hand. This will probably propel the knife right through the head and into the board below, but all you need to do is penetrate about one inch. Although dead, the tail may give a few convulsive flaps on entering the water, so mind you don't get splashed. A scalded hand greatly reduces your enjoyment of the subsequent feast.

Use sufficient water to cover completely all the lobsters you are cooking. Drop the lobsters into the water and bring it back to the boil and simmer for six minutes for lobsters of one to one and a half pounds and eight minutes for larger ones.

Preparing

Do not leave the lobster standing in hot water after cooking time. Drain and immerse in cold water for a few minutes, place on the draining board the right way up and leave to drain for 20 to 30 minutes. Now either dress and eat or dress and store chilled in a sealed container, or bag whole and store in the refrigerator to dress later.

Do not eat lobster or any other shell-fish too cold as this greatly reduces the flavour. Remove from the fridge about an hour before eating, but keep covered until served.

The term 'to dress' a lobster or crab has always struck me as being the reverse of what you wish to achieve. To extract the flesh from the shell you will need the following equipment:

- ☐ A wooden or plastic chopping board
- ☐ A sharp, stiff knife with about an eight inch blade

- [ ] A very thin-bladed small knife

- [ ] Something heavy to crack the thick shell of the claws. For this I use the handle of an all stainless steel dinner knife, but a toffee hammer, or pair of nut crackers or the one pound weight from the kitchen scales will work equally well.

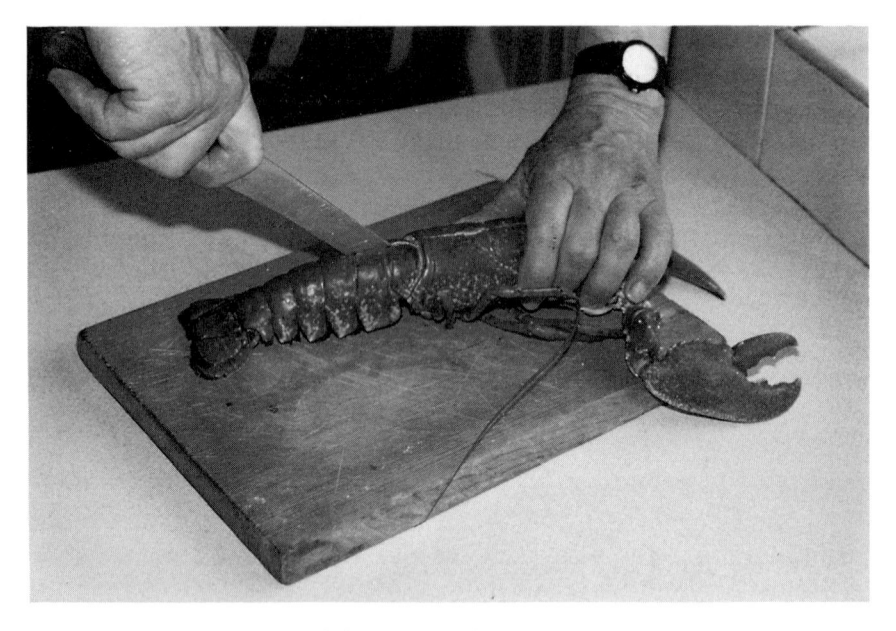

Lobster preparation, stage 1

Pull the large front legs off where they join the body and place on one side. Place the body on the board, the right way up, take the long-bladed knife and insert the point into the cross of the two lines on the back, with the cutting edge facing the tail and the tail facing you. Hold the body forward of the knife and press the blade, point first, right through to the board. Cut the body in half, right through to the tip of the tail. Cut through the head to the spike at the front and pull the lobster into two halves. Rinse away the obvious stomach contents under a gently running tap.

Now pull the body contents and the tail meat out of the half shell. Pull the tail meat away from the body contents if it has remained attached. Pull the small legs off and place aside. Discard the body contents, retaining if you wish any bright red roe, known as the coral. I do not find this particularly good to eat, but it makes a bright garnish or can be used to colour and help flavour a sauce.

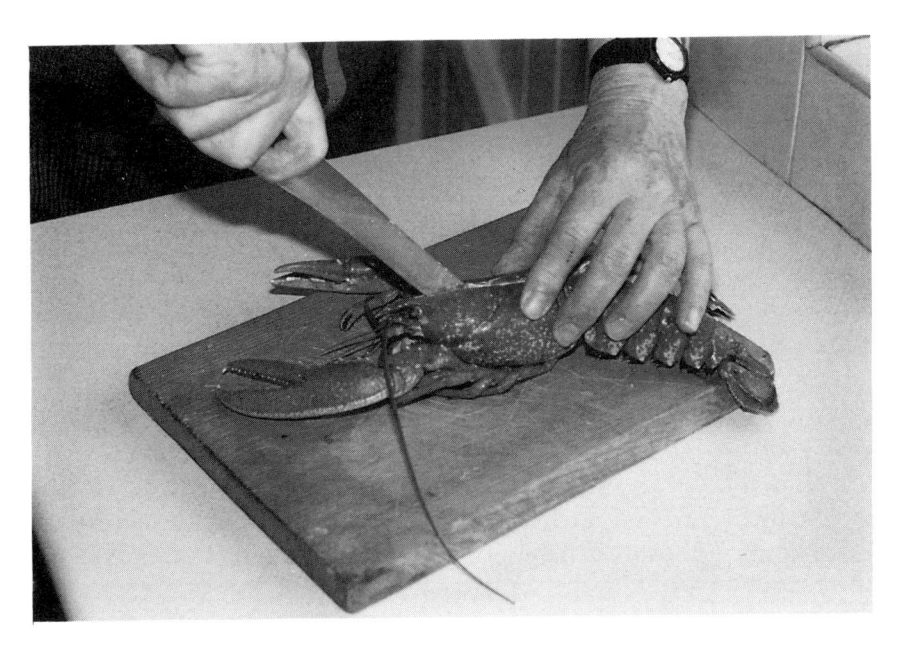

Lobster preparation, stage 2.

When the body contents have been removed from the main shell there is often a white creamy substance adhering to the inside of the shell. This is good to eat. If you wish to use the half shells for presentation purposes, clean them with a stiff brush under running water, pulling away the antennae and mouth parts if you wish.

Take the half tail meat and rinse under running water to remove any stomach contents that have adhered to the front end. A portion of the tail meat extends forward into the main shell and this protrusion may be stained yellow or greenish grey by the stomach contents. This is perfectly safe to eat, but I cut it away for aesthetic reasons.

Similarly, I remove the gut, which is a fragile, semi-transparent tube running the length of the tail and culminating in a small sack, known as the cloaca. If you have been very accurate in halving the tail, bits of the gut will be in both halves. It is more likely that you will find it intact, just into one half or the other. These finer points are seldom observed in restaurants, which annoys me, considering the price they charge.

If you are going to present the meat in the half shell, place the half tail meat in the opposite half shell from whence they came, so that the red side of the meat is uppermost. Now break the large legs into separate joints and rake the meat out with the small thin-bladed knife or crack them open. If you crack them, be careful not to get slivers of shell in with the meat. The flesh from the small legs can usually be squeezed out of the sections, between finger and thumb. If you find this difficult, squeeze it out between the board and the handle of a knife. Place the leg meat and the cream from the shell into the main shell.

Now take a claw and pull the movable pincer back towards the wrist until you feel a distinct click, then pull out in a forward direction. It should bring with it a bony plate. If it does not, the plate will be found in the centre of the main claw meat. Crack open both portions of each claw. If you do this carefully you should end up with perfect claw-shaped meat to lay across the centre of each half shell. Serve with salad as a starter or main course, depending on size.

For fancy lobster recipes, prepare as above and follow a good cook book. You can batter and deep fry pieces of lobster and use them instead of king prawn tails as a basis for a Chinese sweet and sour dish.

If you wish to be a total Philistine you can have your battered lobster with chips!

Sand Eels

The name 'sand eel' is a misnomer, the correct name being *Launce*. This is a true fish, but so slender that at first sight it really does resemble a small eel.

These little fish are gregarious by nature, living in shoals varying in size from thousands to millions. They swim on or near the bottom over sandy ground, where they can take cover in seconds by burrowing into the sand.

They grow to about a foot in length, at which size they are the thickness of a forefinger. More commonly, they are from four to six inches long and the thickness of a pencil. You will find them in the same sort of area as razor fish, in the last 10 yards of sand exposed by very low tides. They will be buried from half to one and a half inches deep and give no sign of their presence.

Catching

To find them you will need a garden rake which you draw quickly through the surface sand. You will have to proceed by trial and error, raking a few square feet and then moving a few paces. If you locate a good colony you can rake up half a dozen or more on each stroke of the rake. If the sand is wet, they will bury themselves again very rapidly, so you have to grasp them quickly. You will probably catch more with one person raking and another person grabbing them, once you have located them in good numbers.

Transport them in half a bucket of sea water, as they deteriorate in flavour quite quickly, once dead. Cook and eat as soon as possible or prepare and store chilled until the following day.

Cooking and Preparing

To prepare for cooking, pinch off the head and run your thumb along the body, from the tail to where the head has been removed. This will push out the guts. Small ones can be left whole if desired. Wash and leave a few minutes to drain.

Toss in seasoned flour or fine oatmeal and deep fry until crisp. Eat with a squeeze of lemon juice or a dash of Tabasco sauce. If you like whitebait you will love sand eel.

If you are fortunate enough to catch any really large specimens, these can be poached lightly. The tasty white flesh parts easily from the backbone.

Sand eels are oily fish and are, therefore, very beneficial to your health. They have not been commercially exploited for culinary purposes because of the difficulty in getting them to market in good condition.

The Danes have always fished for sand eels, using them for animal feed. Before they could be fed to animals they had to be cooked and most of the oil expressed under pressure. This excess oil was a nuisance as there was no other use for it and it was expensive to dispose of until somebody had the bright idea of burning it in a power station. This idea totally altered the economics of sand eel fishing. The Danes now wanted as many sand eels as they could get and speedily set about getting them. They could not catch enough themselves as they had developed an export market for the fish-meal and were getting paid for all the oil they could produce.

This vastly increased demand for sand eels coincided with the E.E.C. deciding to limit fishing effort for a number of the most popular sea fish. The new sand eel fishery offered the opportunity to divert boats from pressure stock fishing and large E.E.C. grants were made available to convert boats and gear to the catching of sand eels.

Many of our west coast boats took advantage of these grants, particularly in Scotland, as there were huge numbers of sand eels in North Western waters. The Danes positioned large freezer factory ships at the main Scottish west coast ports and bought in the catch directly from our boats pulling alongside.

These Klondykers, as they are known, block freeze the catch and send it back to Denmark on a regular shuttle service.

Initially, fortunes were made and more and more boats converted to sand eel fishing. By the mid 1980s, the catches started to fall, so more effort had to be expended to get good catches. This decimated the stocks and a drastic decline in the breeding sea-bird population was noted. The reduction has been as much as 50 per cent in some areas and many of the birds still breeding have failed to raise their young. This pillage continues, not only affecting our birds, but other valuable species of fish which feed on the sand eel.

If you happen across some sand eels, don't worry about taking a reasonable quantity as this will literally be a drop in the ocean, compared to the commercial catch.

Whitebait

On occasion, large shoals of whitebait come close inshore during the Summer months. These are actually immature herring and in a year's time will grow into sprats and in a further year into small herring.

Some years ago whitebait became very scarce, because of over exploitation of the herring stocks. This has, to some extent, been remedied by the drastic measure of a four-year total ban on commercial herring fishing in the early 1980s and subsequent imposition of strict quotas for E.E.C. members.

Whitebait is now reappearing in reasonable numbers and from the sea birds' point of view, they are a saviour, partially mitigating the sand eel calamity.

The shoals of whitebait swim against the wind and wave, to avoid being washed ashore in rough weather, so you will only find them close inshore in calm weather or when an off-shore wind has been blowing for some time.

When they come close inshore, they are usually followed in by shoals of mackerel. The harrying by the mackerel forces the whitebait into denser and denser masses and into progressively shallower water, until they appear as a nearly solid dark mass only a few paces from the water's edge.

If you wade into this mass it will instantly part and you will find yourself standing in a clear hole in the centre of the shoal. If you keep totally still, they will slowly close back around you.

Catching

To catch them you need a very fine mesh net, say an eighth inch square mesh or less, but not so fine that you cannot lift it through the water fairly quickly. An ideal net is circular, about 18 inches in diameter and about two feet deep. The deeper the net, the easier it is to lift off the bottom, before it starts to drag in the water. The net should have a strong but slim handle about five feet long and the net ring should be bent at a slight angle to the handle, so that the ring lies flat on the sea bed when the handle is extended in front of you. Weight the bottom of the net with small lead weights or place a few pebbles in the net, to make it sink and not billow up through the ring.

Wade out to the edge of the shoal and extend your net and sink it to the bottom. The shoal will part, but if you keep quite still it will re-form over the net. Lift as smartly as possible and you may catch 100 or more in the one lift. If the water is cloudy and the whitebait cannot see the net easily, you can catch them by sweeping it horizontally through the water.

Apart from being close to the water's edge and actually seeing the dark mass of the shoal, there are two good indications of their presence. Gulls and terns may be seen repeatedly diving into the water or human beings may be observed acting in what, to the uninitiated, would no doubt appear to be a most peculiar manner.

On occasion, shoals may become concentrated in deeper water, behind jetties, breakwaters and so on or in small rocky bays. When the water is too deep to use a hand net and you can get to a position above the shoal, a drop net can catch large quantities.

To make one you will need to form a hoop about three feet in diameter. Use a quarter inch iron or other metal bar that can easily be bent to form a hoop. Alternatively, use half inch polythene water pipe, closing the hoop by forcing the two ends on to a three inch length of dowelling. The disadvantage of polythene tubing is that the air trapped inside makes it buoyant. This can be overcome by drilling holes vertically though both walls of the tube about every two inches. This allows the air to escape and the net to sink in a few seconds.

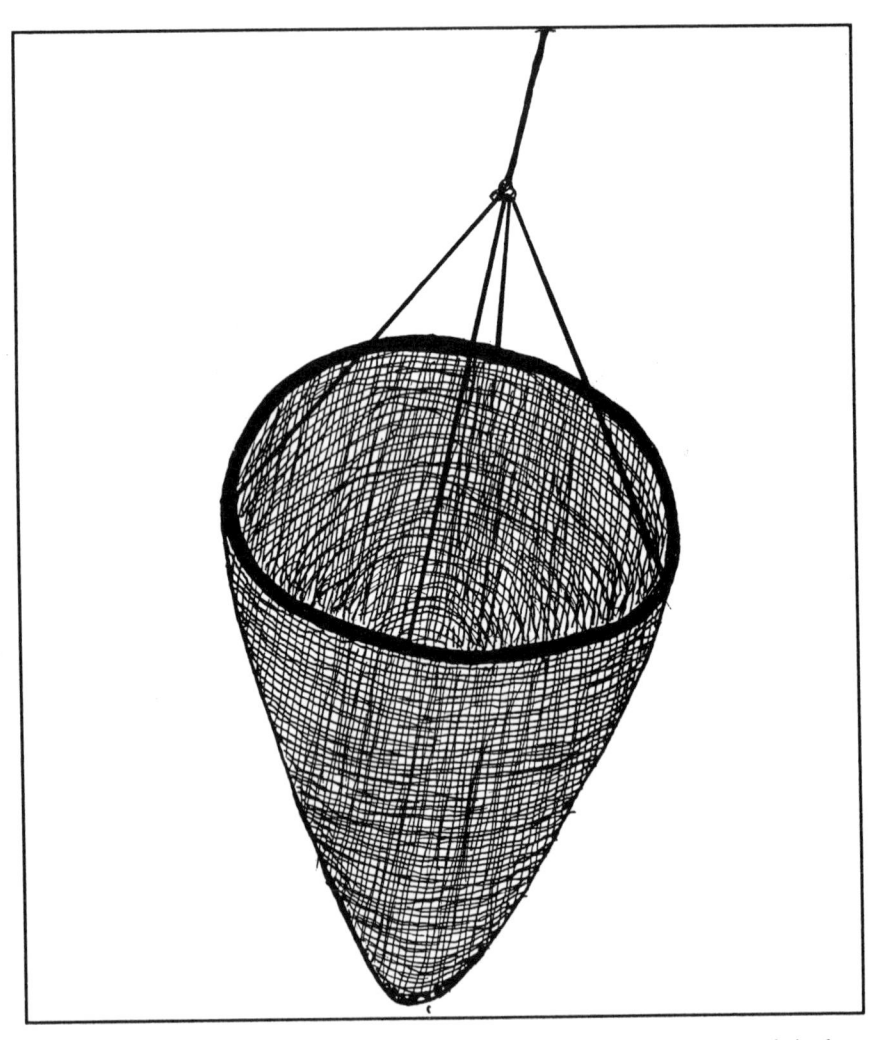

Whitebait Drop Net: diameter three to four feet; depth, similar; the mesh is one-eigth of an inch square or less

Suspend a suitable small mesh net from the hoop. The net should be about three feet deep and weighted in the bottom to assist sinking. If you wish, you can form a tie off sock end to facilitate emptying.

Attach two lengths of strong nylon cord across the mouth of the net at right angles to each other and of sufficient length to form a pyramid above the net. Form a small loop at the centre of each cross cord and attach to these loops a single drop line of thin nylon or corlene rope about 10 yards long.

Drop the net into the shoal and wait for it to close over the net. Lift as quickly as possible to the surface. If the water is deep the shoal will usually only be in the top two or three feet and it will not be necessary to lower the net to the bottom. Lower it only as far as needed to allow the shoal to re-form above it.

Occasionally large quantities of whitebait or sprats are stranded on the tide line. This happens when mackerel have been harassing the shoal and there is some wave at the water's edge. They get driven right into the breaking wave and are thrown on the beach. They die very quickly out of water and are washed progressively higher up the beach by an incoming tide, to be left in a band about a yard wide at high water mark. If they are still damp and smooth, collect them. If they have started to dry and wrinkle, don't bother, as they will be past their best. Whitebait, like sand eels, spoil quickly, so eat or freeze as soon as possible after capture.

Cooking and Preparing

Toss them whole in seasoned flour or fine oatmeal and deep fry until crisp. Season with lemon juice or Tabasco sauce. If you catch any sprats you may prefer to pinch off the heads and squeeze out the guts before cooking, but you will come to no harm eating the lot.

If you want to freeze whitebait or sand eel, assume that you are going to catch some and set the freezer to quick freeze before you set out. As soon as you get home, wash your catch in cold water and thoroughly drain. Spread them out on thick kitchen tissue or other absorbent material and pat them with more tissue, until reasonably dry. Spread them out, no more than two deep on trays and place in the freezer. This will freeze them quickly and separately and they can then be placed loose in a sealed bag or box.

If you freeze them in bulk, they will freeze much more slowly, losing body fluid in the process and will set into a solid block. When you thaw this block, you will have shrivelled bodies and a quantity of useless fluid. Frozen dry and loose, you can remove just as many as you want from the freezer and cook frozen. You will, of course, have to give them a quick rinse to get the flour to adhere.

It is possible, on occasion, particularly with a drop net, to catch very large quantities of whitebait. Please don't take more than you need for family and friends, as the birds have first priority.

Flounders

These tasty flat fish are found in most estuarial waters and for quite considerable distances up slow flowing rivers. While essentially sea fish, they have developed a predilection for living in fresh or brackish water and are tolerant of rapid changes of salinity.

In small estuaries they will be lying in the main channel when the tide is out. In large estuaries, numerous channels and pools may be left when the tide recedes and the flounders will wait in these until the tide returns.

Flounders are extremely adept at camouflage, being able to change their body colour and pattern quite quickly to match the bottom on which they are lying. This makes them difficult to see if the water is clean and nearly impossible if the water is slightly cloudy.

Catching

Catching flounders is, therefore, more of a challenge than a profitable exercise. In clear water your only chance is to spot them before they spot you and stab them with a long handled spear. To redress slightly the uneven balance of this contest, which is weighted heavily in favour of the flounder, I offer the following tips:

Wear polarising sun glasses to improve visibility into the water. Don't waste time if there is a ripple on the water. Preferably go in sunny conditions as this improves visibility into the water, but make sure that your shadow does not precede you.

Move slowly and stealthily, a pace at a time, pausing to study the bottom, before taking the next step. Stab any slight, oval hump in the sand or silt. With practice and after many misses you will start to develop a feel for what might be a flounder lying camouflaged on the bottom.

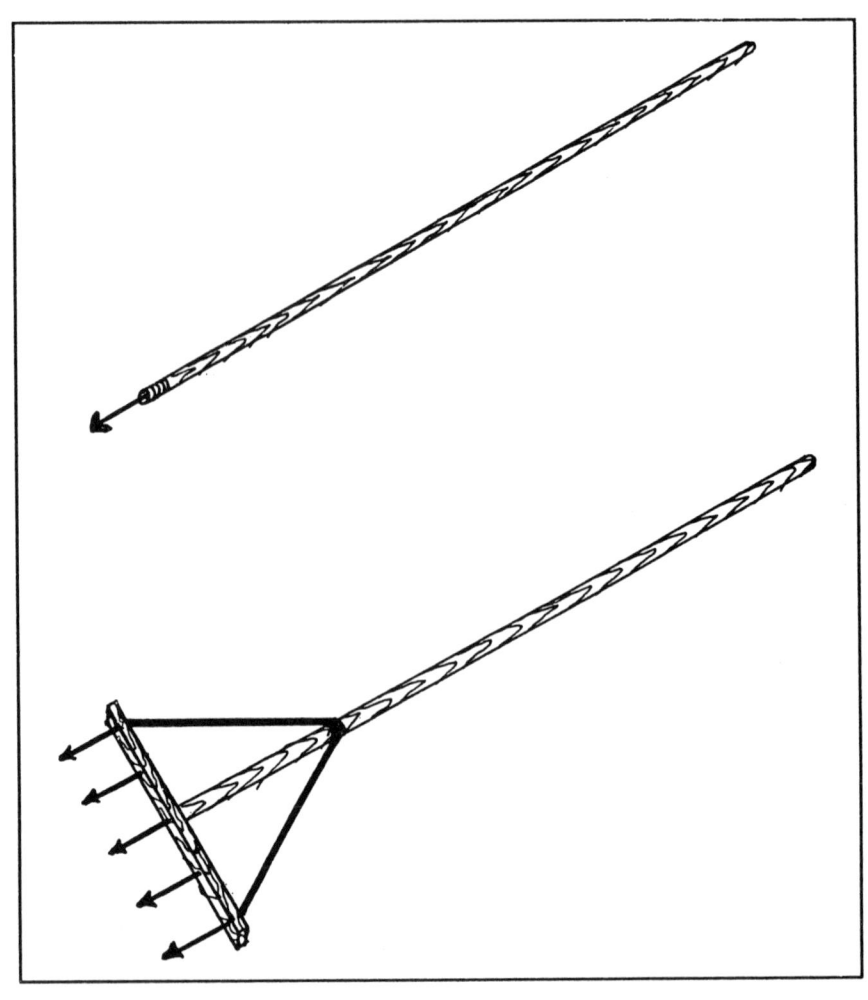

Flounder spears: use a five-foot to six-foot handle of about one inch diameter

Seashore Seafood

Make your spear from a five or six foot length of three quarter or one inch dowelling. Cut the head from a six inch nail and hammer the pointed end until it is well flattened. Heat will make this much easier and if you heat it until cherry red a width of at least half an inch should be easy enough to obtain. File this flattened end into a barbed arrow head shape, but do not form too fine a point, as you will quickly blunt or bend it when it hits the bottom. Round the point and sharpen from each side.

Drill a two inch deep hole in one end of the dowelling and insert the cut end of the nail, together with a little Araldite or other strong glue. Bind the last inch of the wood with copper wire to prevent splitting.

Many flounders will swim away before you have spotted them. The first thing you will see is a rapidly extending trail of disturbed sediment. If you stand still you may, in shallow water, be able to see where it settles.

If the water is cloudy or if the flounders are disguised by a covering of silt which makes them virtually invisible, random repeated stabbing has to be employed. In this method a multi-pointed spear greatly increases the chances of success.

In cloudy water the flounders will be unaware of your presence if you proceed quietly and will not swim away. Stab about two feet ahead and then to the left and right. Move forward about two feet at a time.

Flounders grow to well over a foot in length and a weight of two pounds or more. Those of six inches or less are not worth keeping as there is little flesh on them, but if you catch small ones accidentally, take them home for the cat,. Do not return them injured.

A friend of mine catches many good flounders by paddling around the muddy channels in our local harbour wearing a discarded pair of spiked golf shoes. When he has one trapped underfoot he bends down and feels for the head, lifting it from the water by pinching it in the gills between forefinger and thumb.

I hope you enjoy success. It really does satisfy the old stalking and hunting instinct, without giving you problems from the anti blood-sports brigade.

Cooking and Preparing

A really good specimen can be filleted, while smaller ones are better cooked on the bone. With a sharp knife or scissors, remove the head and guts and cut off the tail and side fins, starting from the tail end.

Poach, fry or brush with oil and grill.

Occasional Discoveries

The preceding pages have covered the species that are common or reasonably common and you can expect to find by visiting the right locations.

Apart from these, occasional, unexpected bonuses can occur. Shallow, tidal pools have been known to yield codling, place, sole, turbot and on one occasion in my area, a 14 pound salmon.

This fish should, of course, have been left unmolested, as the unlicensed taking of salmon and sea trout, even in the sea, is an offence under the Salmon and Freshwater Fisheries Act. The lucky finder of this specimen was not apprehended and later claimed to be totally unaware of the provisions of the Act. This is odd, to say the least, as he is a retired policeman.

After strong onshore storms, particularly if they coincide with very low tides, species not normally found can be washed inshore from deeper waters. When there has been a storm of this nature it can be quite rewarding to walk the high water mark at or just after high tide.

In my area I have found whelks, King cockles, horse mussels, scallops, oysters, spider crabs, dogfish and conger eel.

Whelks

These are large sea snails, up to four inches in length and usually grey brown in colour. The flesh is white with varying black blotches. Many people find them good eating, others turn green at the thought.

A different species, with a more elongated shell, a yellow coloration round the opening and an operculum shaped like a comma, is not good eating. If you are not sure, cook them and check the flesh. If it has black blotches it is a whelk, if it is all white it is not.

Whelks in natural habitat

To cook, drop into boiling water, return to the boil and simmer for 15 minutes, drain and allow to cool.

Remove the meat from the shell by gently pulling it with one hand and at the same time twisting the shell with the other. If the soft brown stomach comes out with the meat, pinch this off. Rinse the meat to remove traces of stomach contents and pinch off the long syphon tube if you do not fancy it.

Eat fresh with salt and vinegar to taste or pickle and store by placing in sealable heat proof jars and covering with boiling, plain or spiced pickling vinegar. Seal tops immediately.

There has always been a small market for whelks in the London area and a good demand on the Continent. In recent years the Japanese and South Koreans have developed a considerable liking for them and thousands of tonnes per year are now processed here, frozen and exported to the Orient.

Normally they are cooked, sorted and frozen, but the Japanese also like them raw, serving them thinly sliced with other raw seafoods.

The British fisherman receives between £1.50 and £1.80 per stone for his whelk catch. In a Tokyo Sushi Bar a customer may pay £10 for one thinly sliced raw whelk.

King Cockles

Large deep water cockles are sometimes found. These come in two types, one with deep ridges running round the shell and the other with a very ribbed, rough, spiky shell. They can both vary in colour from off white to dark blue grey. These are not commercially harvested in this country as collecting them involves harrowing and dredging the sea bed which damages the marine environment.

Many continental boats do, however, practise this pillage, taking all sorts of shellfish and other sea-bottom living creatures. Their dredges have spring-loaded spikes which penetrate the sea-bed for up to six inches, burying and killing countless millions of small creatures, many of which form the staple diet of our more popular types of sea-fish, such as plaice and cod.

If you are fortunate enough to find a few, cook as for common cockles. Slightly stronger in flavour, each meat is a mouthful.

Horse Mussels

These are large, deep water mussels, up to about four inches in length, with much bluer shells than common mussels. Cook as ordinary mussels. The meat is usually yellow to orange in colour, firmer and has a stronger flavour. The inside of the shell is often an iridescent mother-of-pearl. I have never found a pearl in one, but would imagine it would be a good one, if I did.

Scallops

The fan-shaped shell depicted on the Oil Company logo. They come in two varieties, the smaller or Queen Scallop and the larger or King Scallop. Both are delicious to eat. The shells vary greatly in colour, from pale cream to dark red brown.

Do not cook in the shell. Prise the two halves a little apart with the tip of a stout knife and insert a sharp blade along the flatter half shell and sever the large white muscle from the shell. Remove the flat half shell, then sever the white muscle from the deep half shell. Retain the white muscle and the orange and cream foot. Discard the rest of the contents.

In a queen the muscle will be about the size of a 1p piece by about quarter of an inch thick. In a king it can be a fair bit bigger than a 50p piece and an inch thick.

Fry the muscle and the foot in butter, for a couple of minutes each side. The foot has a fishy taste while the muscle is half way between a tender steak and a chicken breast.

The flat shells make excellent decorations and the deep half can be used to serve the cooked scallop or to present other dishes. For other recipes see a good cookery book.

Oysters

There are few wild oysters left around our coasts. Those you buy are farmed and are not usually natives, but the very frilly Pacific Oyster, which grows more quickly than the native, has the advantage that it does not breed in our cold waters, so is edible at any time of the year.

Occasionally, however, the sea yields up one or two wild native oysters after a big storm. You can tell the beaches where you may find them by the presence of half oyster shells along the high water mark. One weighing nearly three pounds was washed ashore on one of my local beaches in 1985. This weight is misleading, as it was nearly all shell, the meat inside only being the size of a good fried egg.

Prise off the flat half shell with a stout knife blade, severing any connections. Sever the meat from the deep half shell, retaining as much of the fluid as possible. Swallow whole or chew a couple of times before swallowing. Sprinkle with lemon juice if desired.

Spider Crabs

Among the outer rocks you will often find small spider crabs with bodies up to about the size of a hen's egg, covered in small spikes and with seaweed growing on the shell. They have long, spindly legs, hence the name.

Spider crab

In deeper water these can grow to considerable size, with a body the size of your two hands cupped together and legs over a foot long. The one shown in the photograph spans 27 inches, when spread-eagled.

There is little worth eating in the main shell and as the legs are so slim, you need a good sized specimen to make it worthwhile cooking. The white meat in the legs and claws is very tasty, but you will only get enough for one person from a large specimen.

Occasionally a large one wanders or gets washed inshore, but they are quite often caught in commercial tangle nets laid on the sea-bed to catch flat fish. As there is no market, the fishermen throw them away. If asked, I am sure they would keep you a good specimen or two. Stress that you want them undamaged and offer to pay for them, as it can take up to 10 minutes to extricate one undamaged from the net. Normally the fishermen crush them and pull them out of the net in pieces.

Dogfish

On really low tides various fish can become stranded among the rocks and seaweed.

The most commonly found is the lesser spotted dogfish, less often the greater spotted dogfish or bull huss. The lesser spotted is pale grey brown with black spots and grows to about two feet in length. The bull huss is much darker brown with larger and often more numerous black spots and grows to about 12 pounds in weight.

The lesser spotted is sold as Rock Eel and the bull huss as Rock Salmon. Neither is a quick swimmer and can easily be caught by hand or with your net, when in shallow water. They will wriggle and writhe violently when first caught. Subdue them by grasping by the tail, give them a good swing and clout the head on a convenient rock. Their skin is smooth when rubbed from head to tail, but like very sharp sandpaper when rubbed the other way. Be careful when they are thrashing about as you can easily get a nasty graze from this rough skin.

Before the invention of sandpaper the skins were cured and known as shemine, the coarseness or grade depending on the size of the fish from which it was taken.

Both species have firm white flesh and no small bones. The worst job in preparing them is removing the tough skin. This is best done with the smaller specimens by nailing through the head to a wooden board or post, cutting through the skin right around the fish a little way behind the front fins and splitting the belly from this cut down to the vent, removing the guts. Start cutting away the skin from the flesh around the neck until there is enough free skin to get a grip with a pair of pliers. Pull downwards towards the tail and the skin should come off like an inverted sock. Cut off the head and tail and cut the body into handy sized portions and cook on the bone.

For larger specimens it is easier to cut a fillet from each side of the fish and to remove the skin from the fillet by placing it skin down on a flat surface and pushing a sharp knife forward along the skin, starting at the tail end. Hold the skin firmly in one hand, pulling it towards you and push the knife forward at the same time. The white flesh will have a dark red layer close to the skin. This turns brown on cooking and is quite edible.

To cook, poach in milk and water, pan fry or batter and deep fry.

Conger Eel

While exploring holes under rocks for crabs and lobsters you may well disturb a conger eel. These can grow to enormous size, but among the tidal rocks one of 15 pounds is as large as you are likely to find.

If there is much water around the rock it will be almost impossible to catch, but if the rock is clear of the water you may well be able to hook it out. It will thrash about wildly and is very slippery.

A 15 pounder is about four and a half feet long and about as thick as your leg. They are the very devil to kill and should you wish to keep it, kill it you must. The only way is to club it a number of times on the top of the head with a large stone and drag it up the beach by inserting the tip of your lobster hook into its gill slots.

Skin by suspending from a nail or by impaling on a large meat hook attached to a convenient beam or branch. Cut and gut as described for dogfish, but you will find that the body cavity extends some way beyond the vent. Pull the skin off using two pairs of pliers. The inside of the skin is a pale silver blue. In the past eel skins were used to bind and support sprained joints and broken bones, hardening as they dried, to form a protective case nearly as effective as Plaster of Paris. Their odour, however, left something to be desired.

Cut the body into steaks and either poach in milk and water or pan fry. It is a firm white flesh, with a distinctive taste, often used in France as one of the components of Bouillabaisse, where the head, skin and backbone are also used to boil up to form the stock.

I have found conger very prone to cod worm. These harmless but unpleasant looking parasites are curled up in the flesh, usually in the thinner flesh of the belly flap. They appear as a brown blob, but uncurl and move slowly when removed from the raw flesh. Hold the flesh up to a strong light and they are easily seen. Either remove from the flesh or discard the flesh from the affected area if you are of a squeamish disposition.

They are not in a breeding condition while in fish, so there are no eggs present in the flesh. They mature and reproduce in the gut of seals that have eaten affected fish. Their eggs are voided by the seal, sink to the bottom and are subsequently ingested by fish, so completing the cycle.

Seaweeds

While most seaweeds are edible to some degree, their flavour, texture and appearance do not readily tempt the palate.

But we all eat far more seaweed than we realise. Vast quantities are gathered and in some places to be farmed and processed to extract alginates. These are vegetable gelatines, which have a wide commercial application in processed food, being used in jellies, thickening of soups and sauces, as emulsifiers in ice-cream and to produce the edible sausage skins used today in place of the outer skin of a pig's intestine.

Carragheen

If you wish to experiment and make a vegetarian jelly, look for Carragheen, otherwise known as Irish Moss. You will find this mainly on Western and some Southern shores, adhering to rocks from about the half tide mark outwards. It is best gathered young in April, May and June. It grows as clusters of purplish brown fronds a few inches long, narrow, flattened and multi-branching, quite often forming a fan or flattened tree shape. Sometimes the tips display a bluish iridescence, especially when still submerged.

Thoroughly wash to remove salt water, drain and chop. Place eight ounces of weed with 20 ounces of water into a pan and simmer until the weed has almost disintegrated. Strain off the liquid and allow to stand for a little while. Decant off the clearer liquid from any sediment which has settled. While still hot, add sugar, food flavouring and colouring to taste. Pour into a mould and allow to set.

Laver

The most commonly eaten seaweed in this country is Laver. This grows in numerous places around out coastline, being more abundant in the West.

In South West Wales (and elsewhere) it is regularly gathered for making what is known as Laver bread and this or the uncooked weed can be bought at some shops in that area.

It can be found at various levels of the shore, adhering to stones, particularly those nearly buried in sand. Its thin fronds form an irregularly shaped translucent brown to purple membrane, resembling a frilly lettuce leaf. It is best picked while still suspended in the water, as it has a tendency to pick up sand when it collapses as the water recedes.

Wash thoroughly and place with a little water in a steamer or into a sauce pan. The Laver tends to stick in a saucepan, so simmer gently and stir regularly until it forms a mush, like well-cooked spinach. This can take a considerable time, sometimes as long as three or four hours, but more usually about an hour - depending on the age of the weed.

Chop into a rough paste and drain off the surplus liquid. This cooked pulp is what is known as Laver bread. It will keep chilled in a covered container for three days. Usually eaten at breakfast, it is formed into small flat cakes, coated in oatmeal and fried in bacon fat.

In Japan and China, Laver is extensively cultivated for use in soups and stews, pickles and preserves and for wrapping rice balls.

Dulce

The only other seaweed worth trying is Dulce. This is found on the middle to outer rocks, growing in clusters four to eight inches in length. It is flat, smooth, often branched like a hand and has a deep purplish red colour. Like most seaweeds it turns green when cooked. If you have good teeth, it can be eaten raw or slightly blanched, as a salad vegetable, or the fronds can be fried in hot bacon fat until they start to crisp.

I think it was Sir Thomas Beecham who said that anything was worth trying once, with the possible exceptions of incest and Morris Dancing. You will have to make up your own mind about seaweed.

Snorkelling

One of the problems with the tidal cycle is that the lowest tides occur in the Spring and the Autumn. On Summer low tides some of the best rocks are still covered by three or four feet of water. You can wade to this depth, but it is very difficult to probe under the rocks without getting totally wet and it is very hard to see and catch anything that is under the rock or swims out from beneath it, as your face is so near the water, you can't see clearly into it.

If the water is warm enough and you are a reasonable swimmer, try using a mask and snorkel. This accepts the inevitable that your are going to get soaked, but enables you to probe more easily and to see clearly and follow anything of interest which pops out.

Unless the water is reasonably warm, I would recommend the use of a wet suit, as without one you will not be able to stay in the water long enough to achieve very much.

Restrict your operations to a depth that you can stand up in, with your arms and shoulders clear of the water, or you will have great difficulty in handling anything you catch in your net.

How to retain your catch also poses a problem. An inflated inner tube of suitable size is the answer. Either fit a well perforated plastic bucket tightly into the ring of the tube or suspend a net bag from it. Attach the tube to your waist with a length of thin rope to prevent it drifting away and to leave you with both hands free. In an emergency it will make a good flotation aid.

If there are any lobster pots about, keep clear of them, as it is an offence to remove lobsters or crabs from pots and even if you have caught yours legitimately, you may have difficulty in persuading an angry lobster fisherman of your innocence, if you have been close to his pots.

Flounder stabbing in water over three feet deep is much easier while swimming on the surface looking down and with a six foot handle to your spear, you can stab flat fish resting on the bottom in water up to about eight feet in depth. The fish are far less disturbed by somebody swimming over them, than by wading.

If you are swimming, rather than deep wading, remember to keep a regular check on your position, as it is easy to become absorbed in the hunt and cover a considerable distance. Against a wind or tide, getting back may be far harder than going out. It is also advisable not to snorkel unaccompanied.

Setting Shore Nets

The public has an ancient right to set shore nets for sea-fish, between high and low water marks. No licence is required to do this, but there are some restrictions, designed to protect vulnerable stocks in certain areas.

The Area Sea Fisheries Committee may declare the shore-line between two easily identifiable land-marks, a conservation area. This restriction is usually applied to areas where bass are known to gather to breed.

Under the Salmon and Fresh Water Fisheries Act it is an offence to set nets with the intention of taking salmon and sea trout in fresh or salt water. It is also an offence to retain any salmon or sea trout accidentally taken in the legitimate netting of sea fish. If you do accidentally catch any salmonids, these must be returned to the water with as little damage as possible. They must be returned, even if dead. The offence occurs when you bring or obviously intend to bring, the fish ashore. The excuse that you were bringing the fish off the beach to hand to the police or the National Rivers Authority bailiff will not be accepted.

Certain areas near the estuaries of salmonid rivers are designated Red Areas, where nets may not be set for either all or part of the year. Any area not a Red Area is a Green Area for either all or part of the year.

If the N.R.A. bailiffs observe legally set nets in a Green Area taking an unacceptably high number of salmonids, they may declare all or part of'that Green Area, a temporary Red Area.

Detailed information on areas and applicable dates is obtainable from the N.R.A. Area bailiff or directly from the N.R.A.

regional office, by telephone or letter. Ignorance is not accepted as a defence, but may be taken into account as a mitigating circumstance when considering sentence.

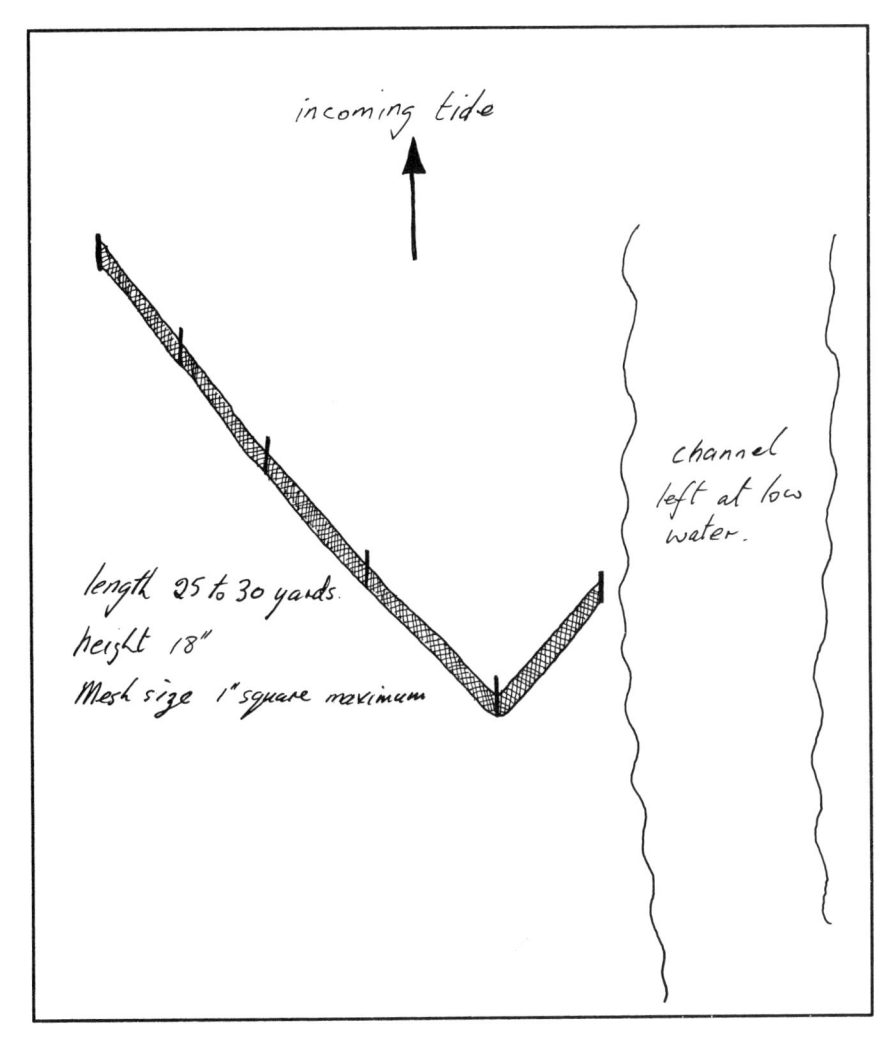

Flounder set net

The most desirable fish to be caught in shore nets is the bass and the capture of this species accounts for the setting of most shore nets. The reasons for this are two fold; bass habitually hug the shore-line and they fetch two or three times as much per pound as salmon. They fetch this high price because of their excellent firm white flesh and the difficulty in catching them, as they spend the greater part of their lives in water too shallow for the commercial fishing boats.

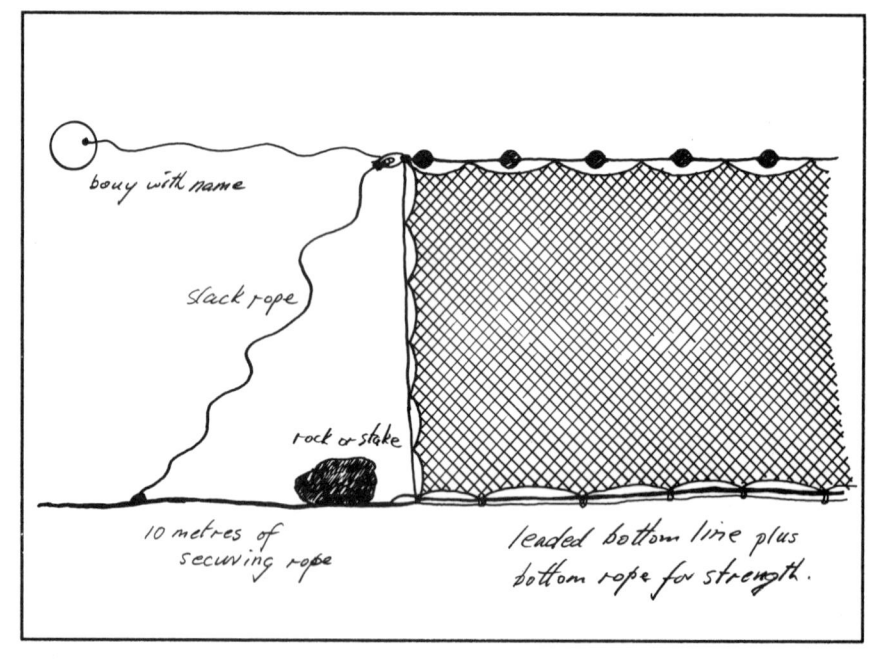

End rigging of bass net

A ready rigged 50 metre bass net should cost you between £50 and £80, depending on quality. They are advertised in Fishing News, which can be ordered from any Newsagent or you can find net manufacturers in the Yellow Pages for most coastal areas under the headings Net Manufacturers or Suppliers.

A bass net has a floating top line and weighted bottom line, with one to one and a half fathoms (six to nine feet) of net suspended loosely between these lines. The net may come to you with securing lines to both ends. If not, attach a 10 metre length of 10mm or 12mm rope to each end of the net, rigged as shown in the diagram.

Set your nets at low water on the three days running up to the lowest tide, securing the outer end as far out as you can reach and lay the net in a line running more or less straight inshore. Firmly secure the inner end. In sandy locations this can be done with either sand anchors or wooden stakes, driven well in. Metal stakes must not be used as these constitute a hazard to navigation when submerged.

On rocky ground, the tail ropes can be secured around rocks and other rocks placed on the ropes for added security. If the net is stretched over rocks it may be necessary to place small rocks on the bottom line to ensure that it follows the bottom contours. Do not set nets in rough weather or if it is forecast to turn rough as this will usually tangle them and fill them with drifting seaweed, the drag of which will damage or move the nets.

If you are setting in a location where a net may be interfered with, stay until it is covered. In any location, return when it is about to start to be uncovered, as gulls and other birds will damage the catch, if left exposed. Check your net on each low tide if possible, as crabs will damage dead fish left in the net.

Dogfish are a nuisance in the net as they curl up into a tangled ball. Whack them on the head to relax them and pull them through the net head first. If your net does get badly tangled or full of seaweed, place the whole lot in a sack and take it home. Fix a stout horizontal bar about eight feet from the ground and pull the net over this, removing tangles and weed and repairing any large holes, The seaweed you remove can go on the compost heap or be dug directly into the soil.

If you do set nets after the day of the lowest tide, do not set the outer end too far out or you will not be able to reach it to release it on the next tide.

If you inadvertently catch a salmon or sea trout, resist the terrible temptation to take it. The bailiffs may well be watching from a distance and they employ high powered binoculars and telephoto video equipment with night image intensifiers, equal to those used by the S.A.S. Remember also that the size limit on bass is strictly enforced with heavy fines and confiscation of gear being the penalty.

Flounders can be taken with set nets and this is a rather easier and cheaper procedure than for bass. As the tide recedes from estuaries, flounders retreat into the deeper channels, venturing forth and spreading out over the silty, muddy, flat areas as the tide returns.

Any net from one to two inch mesh is usable and only needs to be about two feet in height and 25-30 yards in length. It is more productive to use three or four nets of this length than one long one.

Set these nets where you think flounders are likely to forage when the tide is in. Fix the net at an angle of about 45 degrees to the tidal flow, attaching it to wooden stakes driven into the sand or silt at about five yard intervals, stretching the net taught to a height of about 18 inches and burying the remaining six inches of net on the side facing the ebbing tide. Turn the last three or four yards of the net at right angles to the main run, facing into the ebbing tide.

Your net should now look like a giant tick, with the angled end where the water will recede last. The flounders will work their way past the net on the incoming tide, but get trapped in the angle as they fall back on the receding tide. They may well bury themselves in the sand or silt when trapped, so check all along the base of the net, especially in the angle.

As this net is specific to flat fish you can get permission to set it in estuarial waters where other types of net would not be allowed. If salmon and sea trout are known to be present, use a mesh of one and a half inches or less to avoid accidentally gill netting them. Seek permission to set flounder nets in Restricted Areas by applying in writing to your local Sea Fisheries Committee.

By-laws

These are the By-laws in relation to set or stake nets or lines:

a Metal stakes shall only be used under the written authority of the committee.

b The site of the stakes, net or line shall be marked by substantial buoys, non-metallic poles or perches visible above the surface at any state of the tide and such buoys, poles or perches shall be maintained as long as the stakes are in position.

c The owner's name, vessel number or other identifying mark shall be clearly displayed on or attached to at least one buoy, pole or perch.

d No portion of a stake net shall be nearer the centre of any steam or channel than the edge of such stream at low water of the tide during which the net is fishing.

e No portion of any net shall be nearer than 137.5 metres to any portion of another net, not being a hose net or moored whitebait filter net.

f No net shall exceed 275 metres in length.

On written application to the committee, the restriction in (e) above may be waived or reduced for flounder nets.

In addition to the above by-laws there is a prohibition on the use of any gill or enmeshment net with a mesh size between 65mm and 89mm proceeding in a clockwise direction around the coast, from Donna Nook in Lincolnshire on the East Coast to Haverigg Point in Cumbria on the West Coast.

The mesh size of a net is the measurement of the mesh when pulled straight, i.e. the sum of the sizes of two adjacent sides of the mesh. As an example a two inch or 50mm mesh would give a one inch or 25mm square hole.

Seashells

For those who live near the sea or visit the shore regularly, collecting shells can be a fascinating hobby. Around our coast the variety is enormous, but mostly of small size.

There are various books available on British sea shells and I do not wish to duplicate their contents here, but did you know that there are cowrie shells the size of your little finger nail and shells that glory in such exotic names as the Purple Wentletrap and the Pharaohs' Sunset Shell?

You can collect specimens of each species, to see how many you can get and you can collect different sizes and colours of the same species, laying these out in a specimen case, in graduated lines or attractive patterns. Interesting and attractive wall displays can be made by covering a piece of plywood with a dark coloured paper or fabric, glueing the shells to the back board and mounting this display in a picture frame.

To give a reasonable distance between glass and specimen board, edge the board with a thin timber upstand and cover the inside face of this with the backing material. Glue or paste the backing material to the back board and upstand as the weight of the shells, when hung vertically, will cause it to sag.

You can glue little cardboard name tags beneath each species. If you can get these written in copperplate or other old script, using Indian ink and if possible, giving their Latin name, it will start to look very professional. Mounted in a dark oak or mahogany frame it will look like and ultimately become a cherished antique.

Crab and Lobster Shells as Ornaments

A large brown or spider crab shell makes an interesting decoration for the kitchen or study. Scrub the main shell inside and out with a stiff brush under running water and allow to dry. A thin coat of matt varnish will enhance the colour.

If you wish to preserve the whole crab intact you have to be prepared for a fair bit of fiddling work and to display a lot of patience. You can, of course, just place the specimen out in the garden, protected from animals and birds and let insects and bacteria do their work. This method has two main disadvantages: the smell is appalling for some weeks and the legs will tend to fall apart at the joints and away from the main shell, requiring difficult re-mounting.

The method I use is to cook the crab and then carefully separate the underbody, with the legs still attached, from the carapace. Wash, scrub and dry the carapace and put away in a safe place.

Take the under body with the legs attached and remove all the soft parts, including the gills or dead men's fingers. Carefully break open the matrix of thin, white, bony chambers which contain the muscles that control the legs. Pick out as much of the meat as you can, without damaging the leg attachments. Forget about the meat in the legs.

Place the underbody and legs on an oven tray, arranging the

legs in the desired final position and place in a warm oven, set at about 100 degrees centigrade. Leave the oven door just open a crack, the door to the rest of the house closed and the back door and windows wide open. Leave to dry out for about six hours, then remove to a safe place in a dry shed or outbuilding with good ventilation. After a month or two, all odour should have dissipated.

The initial heat drying process can be done in a microwave oven quickly, using three minute heating bursts with, say, 10 minutes drying and cooling periods between, with the oven door open. Continue until there is no evidence of steam when you open the door. This will probably be achieved after about six heatings.

I have found it advisable to carry out the heat drying process when the lady of the house is absent, as the smell of drying crab is rather strong.

A rather more protracted method is to place the underbody and legs outside in dry and, preferably, sunny weather, bringing it in to a dry place at night or if the weather turns damp. This method is preferable to the possibility of a divorce.

When all odour has been dissipated, re-mount the lower body and legs to the carapace using a strong glue or if available, clear silicon rubber sealant. The silicon rubber has the advantage that you can use it in larger quantities than glue, it stays slightly flexible and small quantities can be used to secure any suspect leg joints.

The finished specimen can be varnished if desired and either hung directly on the wall with a length of nylon thread or it can be mounted on a back board, using silicon rubber to secure it.

A lobster can be preserved by the same procedure, but with the difference that you pull the tail away from the body after cooking. Pull the meat out of the tail section and wash out with a strong jet of water. Excavate as much of the body contents as possible via the aperture where the tail was attached. Wash out with a strong jet of water and dry out all the parts by heating as for crab. Remember to arrange the legs in their desired position, before the drying sets the joints.

The tail section will dry quite quickly and will tend to curl up in the process, so lay it flat and weight it down to prevent curl. The two long thin antennae or feelers will also tend to curl up. To prevent this, slide a dry, natural straw over them and arrange them in the desired final position, as it will be impossible to move them when dry.

Reassemble when all odour has dissipated and hang or mount as for crab. Plastic or polystyrene replicas can be bought, but they are expensive and not a patch on the real thing.

Clothing and Footwear

Obviously your choice of clothing will be determined by the time of year and weather conditions.

In warm Summer weather I prefer shorts or swimming trunks and an old pair of tennis shoes or trainers. Ones that cover the ankle bone are ideal, as these protect against scrapes from rough rocks and barnacles. With shoes that do not cover the ankle bone, wear socks and turn these down in two or three layers to cover the ankle.

When gathering or catching on sandy or muddy areas, do not be tempted to do so bare footed. You will sooner or later tread on a sharp piece of stone or sea shell, or some sort of discarded man-made junk.

Another danger on sandy beaches in my area of North Wales, and this no doubt applies to sandy beaches anywhere around our coast, is the possibility of treading on a weaver fish. These are pretty little silver fish, growing to about nine inches in length and having a black dorsal or back fin, the front ray of which is stiff, sharp, erectile and poisonous. This is a defence mechanism to discourage larger fish, birds and sea mammals from swallowing them, but if trodden on with a bare foot, the resulting wound is excruciatingly painful and will need medical attention.

In sunny conditions, unless you are already very well tanned, wear something covering your back. You may well be bending over for two or three hours and very severe sunburn can result. As there is often a breeze on the beach and your attention is occupied you will probably not notice the burning until it is too late.

For gentlemen going a bit thin on top, some form of light hat which will not fall off when bending or blow off easily in a breeze is a wise precaution for the same reason.

In cold conditions wear a number of layers of clothing that you can remove a layer at a time, if you get too hot doing strenuous things.

Wellington boots or thigh waders are essential in cold weather or for venturing into cold water for any lengty period. If you are going to walk any great distance in wellies, remember to put on sufficient pairs of socks to make them a good fit, or your enjoyment may well be marred by blisters.

Hands can be protected from the cold by wearing a pair of large house-hold rubber gloves, with a pair of thin woollen gloves underneath.

The author, suitably attired, with 'Blue' - his constant companion.

More Warnings!

In addition to the warnings given earlier, remember the following points:

- Water is intrinsically dangerous, particularly when cold. Ebbing and flowing tides can cause strong currents, especially when flowing through restricted channels.

- In exploring rocks at the base of cliffs be particularly careful that your retreat is not cut off by the incoming tide.

- When venturing near water or among slippery rocks, it is best to be accompanied by at least one companion, so that you can assist one another in an emergency, or one can go for help if required. If you have to telephone for assistance, dial 999 and ask for the Coast Guard, who will mobilise whichever emergency service is most appropriate. This could be the Lifeboat, Air Sea Rescue, Cliff Rescue or a combination of these services.

- Always tell somebody onshore where you are going and the approximate time you expect to be back. This is particularly important if you are going alone.

- If you are taking children, impress on them not to wander, not to try and run on slippery rocks or climb on to large ones which they might fall off. Try not to let them out of your sight for a moment. Do not wade across channels if you have children with you and be very careful when you do so on your own.

- If you have the misfortune to get stuck in mud, drop to all fours well before it reaches your knees and crawl back the way you have come.

- If you have the even greater misfortune to find yourself in quicksand, throw yourself flat and make flattened breast-stoke motions with your arms and legs. You should, in effect, be able to swim back to solid ground. It is a fallacy that quicksand sucks you down. The human body is slightly more buoyant in quicksand than in water and your head will never sink below the surface, unless you persist in holding your arms above your head.

- If you know the possible problems, heed the warnings, and use your common sense, there is no reason why you should ever have any serious trouble, but remember the Golden Rule, IF IN DOUBT, DON'T.

Not So Pleasant Finds

If you visit the shore as often as I do, you will, over the years happen upon the remains of many dead birds and some animals. The birds will be predominantly sea birds, but the animals will be a mixture of marine and terrestrial mammals. The land animals will have been washed into the sea by rivers in flood, fallen off cliffs or been dumped overboard from ships, when they have died in transit. Some years ago, the body of an elephant was found floating part way between the Orkney Islands and Iceland.

Birds and Mammals

In the case of birds, check for a ring on their leg. If you find one, follow the instructions on the ring, giving date and place of discovery and any other details you may think relevant, such as condition and whether fresh, dead a little while or long dead.

To judge the condition of a freshly dead bird, pinch the breast between finger and thumb, either side of the breast bone. Most dead birds will be emaciated, having died of old age or starvation. If the breast is reasonably plump, it has probably died by accident, usually by being trapped in nets.

Your reward for your trouble will be a letter of thanks from the British Museum, giving details of the species, age and origin of the bird. You will also have the satisfaction of knowing that you have added just a little to the sum of human knowledge.

Dead terrestrial animals such as sheep, goats and cattle (I once found a fully grown red deer) and marine animals such as seals, porpoises and dolphins should be reported to the Environmental

Heath Officer of the Local Council, who have the statutory duty to remove and dispose of such remains where they may cause public offence or be a danger to health.

Humans!

The greatest misfortune of all is to find a human body. This fortunately is a most uncommon occurrence. If you do, touch nothing unless there is the possibility that life is not extinct or the body is in imminent danger of being washed away. Notify the Police or Coast Guard as quickly as possible.

The story is still told in my village of the very forbidding and very strict landlady of the local pub. She was infamous for handing out lengthy bans for the most minor transgression.

There was a local fisherman named Will, renowned for his expertise in his chosen profession and for his capacity for draught Bass. While playing dominoes in the snug, Will inadvertently uttered an expletive and found himself banned from the premises. It was common knowledge that her ladyship, as she was less than affectionately known, seldom relented on such a ban in less than a month.

Will was devastated, as this was in the days when few locals had cars, the last bus went at eight o'clock and the next pub was four miles down the road.

In his melancholy, he took to long walks, much to the relief of his wife and the delight of his dog. On one of these forays along the beach he discovered a corpse wedged between rocks and, not being of a squeamish nature, decided to pull it out from where it was stuck and drag it further up the beach, as the tide was coming in. Later in life he would relate to anybody who would listen, the story of his discovery, observing among numerous other gruesome details, that when he moved the body he found at least a couple of dozen good-sized prawns trapped beneath it.

The discovery did give him a local and short-lived claim to fame. On the night after the discovery, his friends were more than surprised to find him in his usual seat in the snug and her ladyship serving him without any problem. He had, by all appearances, been there for some time and one of the lads leaned over and quietly enquired if it was his discovery that had facilitated his rapid reinstatement. Will smiled as he observed: "I suppose so, you know how much she loves prawns".

Legal Size Limits

These size limits are designed as a conservation measure and are imposed Nationally under The Sea Fishing (Enforcement of Community Conservation Measures) Order 1986 together with Statutory Instruments 1986 No. 496, 1986 No. 497, 1989 No. 919.

Within this legislation, discretion is granted to Area Sea Fisheries Committees to raise their own bye-laws to vary the size limits within their own area for any species they feel needs additional protection within their area.

This legislation is obviously intended to control commercial fishing, but applies equally to the individual on the beach, collecting for his or her own use.

The size limits are set to ensure that the creature concerned has had the opportunity to breed at least once and in some instances twice, before reaching catchable size. The size limits for the species covered by this book are listed on the next page.

To the best of my knowledge and belief, this information is correct as at 1st January 1994 but is intended for guidance only. The by-laws and limits detailed are subject to change, so check each year with your local Sea Fisheries Committee. You will find them most helpful. A telephone call will usually elicit the information you require and on request they will send you, free of charge, a comprehensive list of size limits, together with any local variations, specific regulations governing bass fishing and a copy of the relevant Fisheries bye-laws.

For specific local details of Red Areas for shore set nets contact your local office of the National Rivers Authority.

Seashore Seafood

Winkles	None given.
Cockles	Must not pass a rigid square aperture measuring 2cm x 2cm.
Mussels	Not less than 5.1cm in length.
Razor fish	None given.
Shrimps	None given.
Prawns	None given.
Brown crabs	12.5cm across back
Velvet crabs	6.5cm across back.
Lobsters	8.5cm from back of eye socket in straight line backwards to back edge of carapace. 8.7cm in North-Western and North Wales Sea Fisheries Committee Areas.
Sand Eel	None given.
Whitebait	None given.
Sprats	None given.
Flounders	25cms.
Whelks	None given.
King cockles	None given, but apply common cockle size.
Horse mussels	None given, but apply common mussel size.
Scallops	10cms largest measurement. 11cms in part of North-Western and North Wales area. Cemaes Head to Braich-y-Pwll.
Oysters	None given.
Spider crabs	12cm centre line back to front.
Dogfish	None given.
Conger eel	58cms.
Bass	36cms.
Grey mullet	20cms.

Sea Fisheries Committee Offices

The addresses and telephone numbers of the local Sea Fisheries Committee Offices are given below:

Northumberland SFC
Sun Alliance House
35 Mosley Street
Newcastle Upon Tyne NE1 5JY
Tel: 091 261 1841

North Eastern SFC
County Hall
Beverley
North Humberside HU17 9BA
Tel: 0482 867131

Eastern SFC
10 Tuesday Market Place
Kings Lynn
Norfolk PE30 1LD
Tel: 0553 775321

Kent and Essex SFC
County Hall
Maidstone
Kent ME14 1XQ
Tel: 0622 69427

Sussex SFC
2 Sadler Way
Brighton
East Sussex BN2 5PL
Tel: 0273 680210

Southern SFC
Fisheries Office, 3 Park Road
Poole
Dorset BH15 2SH
Tel: 0202 721373

Devon SFC
Fisheries Office
First Floor, Fish Market and Jetty
Brixham
Devon
Tel: 08045 4648

Cornwall SFC
County Hall
Truro
Cornwall TR1 3AY

Isles of Scilly SFC
Town Hall
St Mary's
Isles of Scilly TR21 0LW
Tel: 0720 22537

South Wales SFC
Queens Building
Cambrian Place
Swansea
West Glamorgan SA1 1TW
Tel: 0792 654466

Northern Western and North Wales SFC
Bailrigg
University of Lancaster
Lancaster
Lancashire LA1 4XY
Tel: 0524 68745

Cumbria SFC
The Courts
Carlisle
Cumbria CA3 8LZ
Tel: 0228 23456

SCOTLAND

The Legislation for and enforcement of Fisheries Regulations in Scotland is dealt with by:

The Scottish Office
Agriculture and Fisheries Department
Fisheries Division
47 Robb's Loan
Edinburgh EH14 1TW
Tel: 031 556 8400

Fisherman's Notebook

Date	Location	Notes

Seashore Seafood

Date	Location	Notes

SIGMA Leisure

We publish a wide selection of guides to individual towns, plus books on walking and cycling in the great outdoors throughout England and Wales. This is a recent selection:

Cycling...

CYCLE UK! The essential guide to leisure cycling – Les Lumsdon *(£9.95)*

OFF-BEAT CYCLING & MOUNTAIN BIKING IN THE PEAK DISTRICT – Clive Smith *(£6.95)*

MORE OFF-BEAT CYCLING IN THE PEAK DISTRICT – Clive Smith *(£6.95)*

50 BEST CYCLE RIDES IN CHESHIRE – edited by Graham Beech *(£7.95)*

CYCLING IN THE COTSWOLDS – Stephen Hill *(£6.95)*

CYCLING IN THE CHILTERNS – Henry Tindell *(£7.95)*

CYCLING IN SOUTH WALES – Rosemary Evans *(£7.95)*

CYCLING IN LINCOLNSHIRE – Penny & Bill Howe *(£7.95)*

CYCLING IN NORTH STAFFORDSHIRE – Linda Wain *(£7.95)*

BY-WAY TRAVELS SOUTH OF LONDON – Geoff Marshall *(£7.95)*

Country Walking...

FIFTY CLASSIC WALKS IN THE PENNINES – Terry Marsh *(£7.95)*

RAMBLES IN NORTH WALES – Roger Redfern

HERITAGE WALKS IN THE PEAK DISTRICT – Clive Price

EAST CHESHIRE WALKS – Graham Beech

WEST CHESHIRE WALKS – Jen Darling

WEST PENNINE WALKS – Mike Cresswell

NEWARK AND SHERWOOD RAMBLES – Malcolm McKenzie *(£5.95)*

RAMBLES IN NORTH NOTTINGHAMSHIRE – Malcolm McKenzie

RAMBLES AROUND MANCHESTER – Mike Cresswell

WELSH WALKS: Dolgellau /Cambrian Coast – L. Main & M. Perrott *(£5.95)*

WELSH WALKS: Aberystwyth & District – L. Main & M. Perrott *(£5.95)*

– all of these books are currently £6.95 each, except where indicated

Long-distance walking...

WHARFEDALE TO WESTMORLAND:
Historical Walks in the Yorkshire Dales – Aline Watson

THE MARCHES WAY – Les Lumsden

THE TWO ROSES WAY – Peter Billington *et al*

THE RED ROSE WAY – Tom Schofield

– all £6.95 each

Explore the Lake District with Sigma!

CYCLING IN THE LAKE DISTRICT – John Wood *(£7.95)*

LAKELAND ROCKY RAMBLES: Geology beneath your feet – Brian Lynas *(£7.95)*

PUB WALKS IN THE LAKE DISTRICT – Neil Coates *(£6.95)*

A LOG BOOK OF WAINWRIGHT'S FELLS – Mark Woosey *(£7.95)*

WESTERN LAKELAND RAMBLES – Gordon Brown *(£5.95)*

LAKELAND WALKING, ON THE LEVEL – Norman Buckley *(£6.95)*

MOSTLY DOWNHILL:
LEISURELY WALKS IN THE LAKE DISTRICT – Alan Pears *(£6.95)*

THE THIRLMERE WAY – Tim Cappelli *(£6.95)*

THE FURNESS TRAIL – Tim Cappelli *(£6.95)*

CHALLENGING WALKS IN NORTH-WEST BRITAIN – Ron Astley *(£9.95)*

Pub Walks...

A fabulous series of 'Pub Walks' books for just about every popular walking area in the UK, all featuring access by public transport • A new series of investigations into the Supernatural • Superb illustrated books on Manchester's football teams

– plus many more entertaining and educational books being regularly added to our list. All of our books are available from your local bookshop. In case of difficulty, or to obtain our complete catalogue, please contact:

Sigma Leisure, 1 South Oak Lane, Wilmslow, Cheshire SK9 6AR

Phone: 0625 – 531035   Fax: 0625 – 536800

ACCESS and VISA orders welcome – call our friendly sales staff or use our 24 hour Answerphone service! Most orders are despatched on the day we receive your order – you could be enjoying our books in just a couple of days.